SYCAMORE SHOALS OF THE WATAUGA

SYCAMORE SHOALS
OF THE
WATAUGA

JENNIFER A. BAUER

Published by The History Press
An imprint of Arcadia Publishing
Charleston, SC
www.historypress.com

Front cover: Dedicated in 1976, this re-creation of Fort Watauga was built using archaeological evidence discovered at the site of the original eighteenth-century fort. *Courtesy of Sycamore Shoals State Historic Park.*

First published 2026

Manufactured in the United States

ISBN 9781467159685

Library of Congress Control Number applied for.

Lovingly dedicated to

Abigail, Madison, Allison, Carrie, Julia, and Bobby

CONTENTS

ACKNOWLEDGEMENTS

Over the last several years, during my career with Tennessee State Parks, I kept searching for the time, the focus, and the inspiration to begin writing this book. Without a doubt, it has been a long-time dream. To my family, friends, coworkers, history lovers, and supporters of Sycamore Shoals, I thank you for encouraging me to complete this project. There are also so many of you that I have had the honor of knowing during my twenty-two years at Sycamore Shoals State Historic Park. You have enriched my life and my understanding of the national significance of this site and taught me more than I could possibly put into writing.

Many thanks to all my dear friends for the help you have selflessly shared with me along the journey of writing *Sycamore Shoals of the Watauga*.

To those who reviewed complete or partial chapters, thank you for your varied perspectives, fresh looks, insights on history, suggestions, support, and the sharing of your time: Chad Bogart and Leslie Brockley, Sycamore Shoals State Historic Park; David Doan, Tom Vaughn, and Dalton Wade, Kings Mountain Chapter of the Overmountain Victory Trail Association; Michael Hardy, historian; Tim Massey, historian; Matthew Frye and Wesley Spurgeon, Tipton Haynes State Historic Site; Cody Boring, Rocky Mount State Historic Site; and Matthew J. Mosca, historic paint finishes specialist.

To all of the talented photographic artists, thank you for sharing your images and your eye for beauty, along with organizations that have preserved historic art, documents, and maps: Emry Lee, photographer; Sycamore Shoals State Historic Park; Essyx Exhibits and Display; Tennessee State Library and Archives; Tennessee State Museum; Charlie Rhodarmer, director of the Sequoyah Birthplace Museum; Mark Finchum, PhD, executive director of Tennessee Council for the Social Studies; Michael Byerley; Cory Franklin, Tennessee State Park Ranger; Steve and Susie Ricker; Sheila Steele Hunt; Tim Massey; Matthew Frye and Wesley Spurgeon, directors, Tipton Haynes State Historic Site; Rebecca Moriarity Smith, Rocky Mount Historical Association; and Mike Carpenter, Berry Site Field School. Photos, maps, and illustrations are courtesy of Sycamore Shoals State Historic Park unless otherwise noted.

Thank you for your help with research assistance, for your dedication to adding documentation to historical events, and for lending a listening ear; Chad Bogart, museum curator and historic interpreter, Sycamore Shoals State Historic Park; Leslie Brockley, administrative assistant, Sycamore Shoals State Historic Park; Melodie Daniels, pension records research; Slade Nakoff, William Tatham and John Carter research; Joe Penza, archivist and records clerk, City of Elizabethton; and Ned L. Irwin, Washington County Archives, Jonesborough.

Special thanks to the many historians who came before us: the first authors who wrote detailed books with supporting documentation; those who wrote articles for historical journals focusing on specific people and events; and teachers, libraries, archivists, museums, government organizations, and individuals who have enthusiastically taught and inspired others, along with protecting records, original documents, and art from the past. Of immense value is the highly detailed and sourced research project on the history of Sycamore Shoals prior to the 1976 opening of the state historic park, compiled and written by Pollyanna Creekmore and Murial Spoden. Mildred Korsuch, a historian and friend with a strong interest in history, shared her research with me over many years.

Thanks and admiration to those who are dedicated to conducting archaeological work to enhance our understanding of the past, including the Division of Archaeology, State of Tennessee; Drs. Jay Franklin, Eileen Erwenwein, and students, East Tennessee State University; Dr. Elizabeth Kellar DeCorse, Bradley A. Creswell, and students, University of Tennessee; S.D. Dean, avocational archaeologist; and many more who came before them.

And thank you to those of you who continue to selflessly volunteer to share history with friends, family, coworkers, and visitors to historic events and other venues: Friends of Sycamore Shoals State Historic Park; the cast of *Liberty! The Saga of Sycamore Shoals*; the Washington County Regiment of

North Carolina Militia; the Overmountain Victory Trail Association; the Sabine Hill Social Society; historical associations and other organizations dedicated to specific sites, events, and time periods; and so many others. Let us always strive to share our history with others.

INTRODUCTION

The 250th anniversary of our nation in 2026 celebrates the 1776 signing of the United States' Declaration of Independence from Great Britain. In honor of this significant event, *Sycamore Shoals of the Watauga* has been written to share the stories, struggles, accomplishments, and contributions of the people who settled on the southwestern frontier, along with the Indigenous people who had long inhabited these same lands.

In the 1770s in colonial America, information, people, and products traveled slowly by land and by water. The overmountain people, living on the west side of the Appalachian Mountains, in the vicinity of today's northeast Tennessee, were more isolated than others in the colonies. When Samuel Adams formed the Boston Committee of Correspondence in November 1772, communication became more organized. By the end of 1774, eleven of the thirteen colonies had also formed similar committees.

The British citizens living in the Northeast were becoming dissatisfied with the overreach of King George III and the controls put upon them. Soon after colonial rebellions began in and around Boston over British taxation, many of the people who opposed taxation rose to leadership roles. Influenced by seventeenth-century English philosophers such as Francis Bacon, John Locke, and others, they felt that a person should base their decisions on reason over superstition, using inquiry and facts for better understanding.

This new way of thinking grew and became increasingly prominent for many living in societies that grew out of the Scientific Revolution of the seventeenth century. Francis Bacon, referred to as the father of the scientific method, believed that experimentation and data collection were important in problem-solving and decision-making. His way of thinking influenced others living in the eighteenth century, upholding the need for reasoning and logic.

John Locke's political vision is thought to have influenced the Founding Fathers. Locke believed that protection of one's liberty and private property, separation of powers in government, separation of church and state, and knowledge acquisition based on experience and reflective thought were all imperative to human well-being. His beliefs on the origins and limits of legitimate governmental authority became an inspiration for the Declaration of Independence. His work also influenced the writing of the United States Constitution.

The Scientific Revolution was followed by a philosophical and intellectual movement, the Enlightenment, also called the Age of Reason, that continued through the eighteenth century.

The principles of the American Revolution—liberty, equality, the right to self-government, and our natural rights of life, liberty, freedom, and property—appear to be a reflection of philosophical thought during this time with the goal of forming a healthy society in America. The huge distance between the colonists and Great Britain, coupled with the amount of time they had been physically separated, found the American colonists becoming more independent. Their desires for their future did not always match the desires of the Crown.

When the Watauga, Nolichucky, Holston, and Carter's Valley settlements were young, they did not have the protection offered by living in a British colony, nor did they have a government with rules that would manage a newly forming society. They started from scratch, and their organizational needs resulted in their creating a government of their own, called the Watauga Association. Each successive year, the settlements grew, and their ability to self-govern and thrive was evident. When the American Revolution moved to the south, they later found themselves and their militias supporting neighboring colonies against the British.

In bringing this fascinating story together, the books and writings of authors who lived in the early nineteenth century forward were significant primary sources, along with documents now protected in archives. The information that was recorded and preserved close to the eighteenth century and later is invaluable to gaining an understanding of the known people who lived in this period and their contributions to historical events. With this comes an impression of how America and its culture changed from early settlement through the American Revolution.

My research involved reading many books as well as historical research compiled by others, journal articles, pension records, and original documents, along with having discussions with historians on both colonial and Cherokee history. Authors of note include, but are not limited to, Lyman Copeland Draper, J.G.M. Ramsey, Samuel Cole Williams, John Haywood, and Henry Timberlake. Collections of historic letters, pension records, maps, land acquisitions, and preserved written material, many in library and museum collections, along with state records, often provided information specific to individuals and what was taking place around them. The bibliography included at the end of the book documents sources used in the preparation of this book and provides a great deal of information for further research.

What we are able to understand from these many sources helps us to piece together a puzzle of the past lives of people. We're unlikely to ever know every detail of the complete story; there is always more to learn, and questions arise when new information comes forth. On occasion, historic documents filed away in public or individual collections resurface. These moments can add a whole new understanding to a person's life and an added glimpse into the history of the time.

Learning and understanding the past is much like solving a mystery. It involves exploration, gathering data, inquiry, and problem solving. For what we do know and understand about the past, there are many more questions that history lovers hope will someday be answered. It is always an exciting work in progress.

Chapter 1

EARLY EXPLORATION IN AMERICA

As the earliest European explorers and settlers arrived on the North American continent from the fifteenth to the eighteenth centuries, they soon discovered that Indigenous people had long inhabited America's lands. It was unknown how long humans had lived here, but as time passed, there were those who nurtured an interest in learning where and when the first humans arrived.

Many explorers happened upon different parts of North America, such as Danish explorer Vitus Bering. He led expeditions in 1724 and 1741 to a region named for him, the Bering Strait land bridge. The possibility existed that this land bridge may have acted as the first route that brought people to North America during the last ice age, when people could walk across the frozen mass of land. Bering's travels revealed that people lived on both sides of the "bridge" and had been trading and traveling through the strait, which connected the Chukchi Peninsula of Russia and the Seward Peninsula of Alaska for thousands of years. Research in this region continued beyond 1942, with genome sequencing data indicating that Paleo-Americans, direct descendants of ancient Siberians, would have crossed the land bridge.

Evidence and artifacts indicating the presence of early humans on the continent most likely were noticed by explorers and settlers over time and still are to this day. As technological improvements continue to enhance the study of archaeology, new discoveries are always taking place, data is shared between scientists, and new questions are posed regarding previous studies. To date, the number of sites that have been studied is quite significant.

Fossils, stone tools, and dwellings are examples of discoveries that often can be dated and support the continuing story of the "peopling of America."

Between 1932 and the 1990s, the presence of the Paleo Clovis culture, ice age humans who made stone and bone tools to hunt animals, was found in conjunction with a site at Blackwater Draw in Clovis, New Mexico, dated as being inhabited 13,050 to 12,750 years ago. It is the first location where Clovis points and artifacts were found along with extinct Pleistocene megafauna. At this time, the Clovis culture was thought to be the first human culture in America. Archaeological and genetic studies of modern Native Americans and ancient human skeletons have provided further evidence of the presence of the Clovis culture. The discovery of stone tools and bones of ice age animals, such as the mastodon, were dated as having been present prior to the appearance of Clovis culture.[1]

In the mid-1980s, genetic research that dated early humans was first conducted on museum specimens. It is now possible to trace human ancestry and evolutionary history by conducting DNA analysis. Finding preserved human DNA in skeletal remains is rare, but soils in higher latitudes, where it is colder, can preserve readable human DNA for tens of thousands of years. A 2008 genetic study suggested that a single population of modern humans migrated toward the Bering land bridge around 30,000 years prior and later crossed into the Americas approximately 16,500 years ago. Additional archaeological evidence indicated that humans were south of the Canadian ice sheets 15,000 years ago.[2]

Since the late 1970s, researchers have considered the possibility that people traveled along the coastline in what is currently called the Pacific Coast Migration Model, transported by watercraft. Much research has been devoted to this model; additionally, some have proposed an Atlantic coast model.[3]

In September 2021, in White Sands National Park, New Mexico, ancient fossilized human footprints preserved in an alkali flat were studied by U.S. Geological Survey researchers. Seeds in the fossilized footprints from an aquatic plant, *Ruppia cirrhosa*, were dated using radiocarbon dating. The study indicated that the footprints were between twenty-one thousand and twenty-three thousand years old. This implied that humans and megafauna both existed during the last glacial maximum, before the Pleistocene extinction event.

A follow-up study was conducted and published in October 2023 by U.S. Geological Survey researchers to address questions related to the accuracy of carbon dating aquatic plants. They isolated about seventy-five thousand pollen grains of terrestrial conifer pollen and used radiocarbon dating; their data indicated that the pollen's age was statistically the same as that of the *Ruppia cirrhosa* seeds. Gathering additional data, the team used optically stimulated luminescence, which determines the dates that quartz grains were last exposed to sunlight. The results indicated that the quartz had a minimum age of about 21,500 years. This discovery lends support to the Pacific Coast Migration Model based on evidence that humans may have been living below the ice sheets of the Bering Strait.[4]

Research continues at White Sands, with the need for additional data to provide evidence for, or against, the possible age of these footprints. Also of interest is what this discovery could mean regarding our understanding of when people first lived on the North American continent and how they survived in extreme conditions during the last glacial maximum.

Taking a huge time jump forward to the sixteenth to eighteenth centuries, one can only wonder what the expectations of explorers were regarding the presence of human occupation on the North American continent. The explorers' needs were focused on survival, finding resources not available in their homeland, new land for settlements, a desire to learn, and in some cases, a desire for global strength.

France was claiming land as early as 1534, with Spain close behind in 1541. Additionally, Great Britain, the Netherlands, and Portugal also had their sights set on colonization. As European traders, explorers, colonizers, and armies arrived, they interacted and traded with many Indigenous tribes, which in time changed their historic native cultures.

Prior to sixteenth-century exploration, the earliest known explorer in North America arrived in the tenth century, according to evidence found in today's Newfoundland, Canada. Working in the 1960s, Norwegian explorer Helge Ingstad and wife, archaeologist Anne Stine Ingstad, studied this site, which was then believed to be the settlement of Vinland, discovered by Viking explorer Leif Erikson. Since their studies, current archaeological research now focuses on L'Anse aux Meadows, which is believed to be the site of Vinland.

By the mid-sixteenth century, trade routes were disrupted between Europe and Asia, stemming from the control of long-used land routes by the Ottoman Empire. As improvements were made in navigation and shipbuilding, longer journeys by sea became possible, along with opportunities to find new routes. In 1492, Christopher Columbus, an Italian explorer, was commissioned by the queen and king of Spain to find a quicker and more direct route to Asia. When he landed in the Caribbean islands, he believed he had found

India. Later, he was credited with accidentally "discovering" America. In 1501, Amerigo Vespucci, from Portugal, discovered lands along the tip of South America. Believing they were separate from Asia, he named the land Mundus Novus, or the New World, which was subsequently mapped by German mapmaker Martin Waldseemüller in 1507. These discoveries were soon followed by explorers from other countries sailing across the world in search of new lands.

Frenchman Jacques Cartier, commissioned by King Francis I, claimed land in 1534 associated with the St. Lawrence River. This land, running from Canada down into New York, was fondly named New France. Cartier's travels also included trying to find a Northwest passage to Asia, along with gold and other riches. The next year, he sailed up the St. Lawrence River to the rapids near present-day Montreal. He considered the rapids the last obstacle to finding the Northwest Passage, so he returned to France feeling there was no hope. He returned in 1541 to promote the settlement.[5]

Many years later, in 1603, Samuel de Champlain explored the New England coast. As he moved north, he founded Quebec in 1608. In his home country, France, he promoted New France to those interested in immigrating. Of interest is the fact that Champlain believed friendship and positive relationships with Indigenous people were necessary for successful trade. Efforts to foster such relationships proved beneficial to both cultures over time.

Less than ten years after Cartier claimed New France, Spain colonized Florida in 1541. Explorer Hernando de Soto arrived on the west coast of Florida with six hundred men, animals, supplies, weapons, and many vessels. De Soto's goal was to establish settlements, build forts, and search for gold and silver as he explored America. For three years he journeyed through the Southeast, meeting many Native tribes who greeted his armies with gifts and ceremonies. Unfortunately, the Spanish soldiers' response was to burn and loot their villages and enslave and murder many natives. This behavior was quite contrary to that of the French, who were nurturing positive relationships with Indigenous peoples. In addition, Europeans introduced diseases to the Indigenous population to which they had never been exposed and thus had no immunity.[6]

Captain Juan Pardo, another Spanish explorer, led an expedition from December 1566 to March 1567 from the Atlantic Ocean into present-day South Carolina, North Carolina, and eastern Tennessee. His purpose was to find an inland route to a Mexican silver-producing town. The first European settlement in the interior of North Carolina, Fort San Juan, was built by

Fort San Juan excavation at the Native site of Joara. *Courtesy of the Berry Site Field School.*

Pardo at the large Native American village of Joara, a regional chiefdom of Mississippian culture and a major trade center occupied from around 1400 to 1600.

Pardo's second expedition, from September 1567 to March 1568, resulted in the building of five additional forts west of Joara. Moving south along the Appalachian Mountains, his goal was to create a land route to Zacatecas in today's Mexico in order to protect the Spanish silver mines. The Spanish thought the Appalachians were connected to a Mexican mountain range, but they were not, thus putting them at too great a distance from their destination. The people of Joara burned Pardo's six forts later in 1568 and killed all 120 Spaniards except one. Pardo returned to Spain the next year.[7]

Joara was first recorded as a Native American site in the 1890s. In 1986, archaeologists first began exploring Joara via an excavation led by Dr. David Moore, professor at Warren Wilson College, who has continually been the lead archaeologist at this site. Among a host of discoveries, Moore and his team found evidence of Mound Builders, burned huts, and sixteenth-century Spanish artifacts. In 2013, archaeologists confirmed that Fort San Juan was also located at this site.

Archaeological fieldwork continues at Joara, which is now named the Berry site, after the surname of the landowners, and is located near present-day Morganton, North Carolina. The Exploring Joara Foundation partners with Warren Wilson College, offering educational programs to the public.

In the late 1500s, Great Britain entered the North American scene with an interest in countering Spanish dominance in North America and expanding England's power on the world stage. In 1584, Queen Elizabeth agreed to allow Sir Walter Raleigh to establish a British colony at Roanoke Island in what is now North Carolina. In 1587, the colony's governor, John White, went back to England for people and supplies, but on his return in 1590, he found that the colony had disappeared. Many theories have been proposed about what happened to the colonists, but no evidence has come forth to prove them. Roanoke Island is now referred to as the Lost Colony due to the disappearance of its people. Though theories abound, proof of what became of the colonists has yet to come to light.

Later, in 1607, through a charter from King James I to the Virginia Company of London, England established Jamestown in the Colony of Virginia. It was located near the Chesapeake Bay and became Virginia's first permanent settlement under the leadership of Captain John Smith.

The Newfoundland colony was established in 1610, followed by the Plymouth colony in 1620, when British pilgrims sailed on the *Mayflower* and landed at Cape Cod, Massachusetts. Subsequently, the New England colonies were established after the success of Jamestown.

From 1620 to 1644, the Dutch controlled New York and New Jersey as part of the colony of New Netherland, established by the Dutch West India Company in 1624. The company was chartered in 1621 to trade and colonize the Americas, believing colonies would flourish in this atmosphere. In 1664, the colony was captured by the English, including parts of present-day New York, New Jersey, Delaware, and Connecticut.

By 1632, Maryland was granted to Lord Baltimore, and one year later, Williamsburg was founded in Virginia. British colonization continued; the last English colony, Georgia, was established in 1732.

Exploring much farther inland were the French. Father Jacques Marquette, a Jesuit missionary, and Sieur Louis Jolliet, a fur trader from Quebec, traveled the Mississippi River around 1673. The Frenchmen reached Chickasaw Bluff in today's Memphis, Tennessee, where the Natives fed them. Marquette recorded that the Native people had articles from the East, including, "Guns, axes, hoes, knives, beads, and double glass bottles in which they keep their powder....They bought stuffs and other articles of Europeans on the east side"—a reference to the Spaniards on the Atlantic Coast.[8]

Frenchman René-Robert Cavelier, Sieur de La Salle was searching for the mouth of the Mississippi, camping at Chickasaw Bluffs along the way. When he reached the Mississippi delta, he took possession of that country for his king, "In the name of Louis XIV, King of France and Navarre, April 9th, 1682." LaSalle claimed the legitimacy of his action by saying he had the consent of the Shawnees and Chickasaws, "with whom we have entered into treaty," though no written document supported this claim.[9]

James Needham and Gabriel Arthur met in early adulthood and became partners in the fur trade. In 1673, they met Colonel Abraham Wood, who sent them to explore the western frontier, find a water route to the southwest, and establish a direct trading relationship with the Cherokee and the Virginia colony. This would break the Occaneechi Indians' role as a middleman between the Cherokee and the colony.

Samuel Cole Williams, in *Dawn of Tennessee and Tennessee History*, indicates that the route taken by Needham and Arthur to the Overhill Cherokee towns took them from Virginia to an old "Indian Road." This road branched, passing the site of Boone and through a low gap between Zionville, North Carolina, and Trade, Tennessee.

> *Thence it went down the Watauga River past Elizabethton; continued down the Watauga to Buffalo Creek, up that stream still following an old buffalo trail...to the waters of Sinking Creek in the environs of the present Johnson City; thence passing a bold spring on the John Tipton-Landon C. Haynes' estate; thence around the base of Buffalo Mountain, to Boone's Creek and to Long Island.*

From there, the road continued to the Little Tennessee River. Per Williams, Needham and Arthur would have passed the Doe, Watauga, Nolichucky, French Broad, and Little Rivers before reaching the Little Tennessee.[10]

On Needham's return trip, Arthur stayed behind to learn the Cherokee language, while Needham returned to Virginia with the peace treaty and to plan for a third expedition. Arthur became part of the Cherokee culture, marrying a Cherokee woman, adopting Cherokee dress, and joining Cherokee warriors on war parties. Not long after passing the Yadkin River, Needham was killed after arguing with his Occaneechi guide Hasecoll, or "Indian John," who hated the English and later encouraged the killing of Arthur. When Arthur arrived home, he was tied to a stake to be burned; a chief stopped the event by killing a Weesock Native who was about to set fire to the brush around Arthur. Later, in May 1674, Arthur was taken back to Fort Henry by the chief that saved his life.[11]

From the 1750s to the 1760s, the Great Wagon Road became a major route for settlers of Scots-Irish, German, English, and French Huguenot heritage, who traveled in Conestoga wagons. Many journeyed from Pennsylvania into the Shenandoah Valley and continued south along this road. From this known route, other roads branched off to the east and west,

Explorers traveling over frontier lands used the lay of the land and waters to navigate. *Courtesy of Sycamore Shoals State Historic Park.*

Longhunters were prepared to spend long periods of time in the frontier wilderness. *Courtesy of Steve Ricker.*

but the mountains remained a barrier to westward movement from the coastal colonies.

Earlier, in 1716, Royal Governor Alexander Spotswood of Virginia and his Knights of the Golden Horseshoe traveled westward toward the Blue Ridge Mountains, apparently undeterred by the challenge. They crossed the mountains and rode into the Shenandoah Valley. In celebration, they buried a bottle claiming the location in the name of King George I. After their return home, each officer received a gold stickpin shaped like a horseshoe with the words, in Latin, "Thus, it is pleasant to cross the mountains"—hence the name, Knights of the Golden Horseshoe, that followed those who participated in the expedition.[12]

Competition for land, primarily between England, France, and Spain, had been ongoing since the early 1500s. Alliances with Indigenous people became a way in which foreign powers could garner support to acquire and hold their land claims. In 1730, before Needham and Arthur's travels, the British signed a treaty with the Cherokee. It provided for the Cherokee's allegiance to the British, which continued into the French and Indian War from 1754 to 1763, in which the French and the British fought over control of North American lands. Before the end of the 1760s, longhunters and settlers began to leave the southern colonies, traveling west across the mountains in search of land and a new life. With the spread of the white man into tribal lands, the Cherokee and their allies continued to support the British, who were trying to keep their subjects under their control within the thirteen colonies.

Chapter 2

THE CHEROKEE PEOPLE

The Cherokee are also known as Kituwah people, Ani-Kituwah, Kituwahigi, Tsalagi, and ᏣᎳᎩ, written using the Cherokee syllabary. Derived from a Muscogee word, *Cherokee* means "people of different speech"; they are also referred to as the Principal People, or Ani-Yunwiya. Their settlements and hunting grounds in the eighteenth century and before encompassed parts of today's southeast Tennessee, western North and South Carolina, Virginia, West Virginia, Kentucky, northeast Alabama, and northern Georgia. Their hunting territory at this time covered approximately forty thousand square miles.[13]

The Cherokee's earliest ancestors were hunters and gatherers from approximately 2000 BC. They later descended from people of the Mississippian Period (800–1600 AD) and built sacred mounds in areas of settlement. Social hierarchies later developed as their communities established chiefdoms. Their towns, developed during the 1700s, all had independent leaders and a matriarchal society. A principal chief was elected by the Cherokee towns.[14]

The written history of the Cherokee began at the time of European contact, believed to be around 1540 when Hernando de Soto arrived in North America. By this time, the Cherokee had developed an agricultural system and peaceful self-government. Later contact with the British, other Europeans, and the tribes of eastern America as colonization began provided information that was recorded in written works such as letters, diaries, and journals. It is important to note that what was written was through the eyes

The Cherokee are deeply connected to nature and agriculture. Here, an eighteenth-century woman tends her garden. *Courtesy of Cory Franklin.*

of European observers. It was not until 1821, when Sequoyah's syllabary was officially adopted by the Cherokee Nation, that the Cherokee people were able to write and record their own history.

According to studies of Native American language in the 1500s, "Iroquoian Cherokee appears to have been centered in the mountainous regions of eastern Tennessee, western North Carolina, and adjacent areas." Kathryn Sampeck and others from Cambridge University noted this when conducting archaeological investigations into the probable routes of Spanish explorers Juan Pardo and Hernando de Soto.[15]

Modern advances in archaeology, geographic information systems (GIS), and technology, such as ground-penetrating radar and other belowground imaging tools, are commonly used in research at known sites once occupied by Indigenous people. New sites are being discovered and studied on a regular basis, providing new evidence that supports the presence of Cherokee ancestors in the Southeast for several thousand years.

Pre-contact Cherokee is a term that refers to early Cherokee people living in western North Carolina and eastern Tennessee from 1000 AD to 1500

AD prior to contact with Europeans. Archaeologists and anthropologists contend that Cherokee ancestors were settled in these areas during the Late Archaic Period (1000 BC to 900 AD) and into the Woodland Period (1000 BC to 1600 AD). Pottery was introduced during the Woodland Period, along with an increase in cultivation of plants such as corn, squash and beans. There is evidence that squash was one of the first crops introduced, as early as 1000 BC.

Sampeck and others have also studied the material culture of the sixteenth- to seventeenth-century Nolichucky towns, which suggests strong ties to styles of known Cherokee towns, particularly regarding ceramics. Archaeological evidence indicates that these were newer towns and did not survive for long, most likely due to European settlers claiming land in this area. Of interest was that the Nolichucky towns fell along a route that facilitated travel to the Cherokee heartland. [16]

East Tennessee State University Professors Jay Franklin and Eileen Erwenwein, along with Nathan Shreve and others, conducted archaeological and geophysical studies, along with surface collections, at sites along the mid-Nolichucky valley from 2015 to 2016. Their research was supported by the Cherokee Preservation Foundation by way of a grant awarded to the Eastern Band of Cherokee Indians Tribal Historic Preservation Office and Jay Franklin of East Tennessee State University.

This project, compared to earlier studies, indicated a diverse cultural pattern matrix of artifacts ranging from pipe forms common to the Tidewater mid-Atlantic to glass bead types found on several European beaches. Interactions with the Spanish in the sixteenth century were supported by the presence of European artifacts. Through the study of ceramics and pottery traditions, connections were made between types found on the Nolichucky and those in other regions, such as the Watauga, Carolina Piedmont, and Overhill Towns.

Geophysics and related systems allowed for the identification of, for example, house and town patterns. One site of interest lends itself to possibly having been a Spanish-named native town, due to the presence of a plaza and, possibly, a palisade.

> *The addition and expansion of shell-temper potting traditions with design elements reminiscent of Dallas and later Overhill suggest that Native towns on the Upper Holston and/or Lower Nolichucky River may have folded into the Middle Nolichucky settlements during the mid-to-late sixteenth century. Given the size of the settlement, shifts in the shell-tempered ceramic*

> *traditions, and the temporal fits between the Middle Nolichucky's ending with the beginning of the Overhill Cherokee, it appears that an emergent regional Overhill identity had taken shape by the late sixteenth and early seventeenth centuries.*[17]

The Overhill or Upper Towns were one of three known Cherokee settlements in the colonial period. Archaeological studies, such as those mentioned earlier, often provide valuable evidence that helps answer questions about the past.

The Lower, Middle, and Upper (or Overhill) Towns were in southeast Tennessee and western North Carolina. The Cherokee refer to their lifeways as units; thus, the different towns each had their own units of military, political, and religious lifeways. The Lower Towns were located along the Savannah and Tugaloo Rivers and the headwaters of the Keowee River. The Elati or Eastern dialect was spoken here until the late nineteenth century. The Middle Towns, the center of the Cherokee Nation, were in the Smoky Mountains of western North Carolina, located along the Tuskasegee and Little Tennessee Rivers, which is where the Mother Town of Kituwah was located. The people of the Middle Towns spoke the Kituhwa or Eastern dialect, which continues to be spoken by many Cherokee on the Qualla Reservation. The Upper Towns, or Overhill settlements, in East Tennessee, followed the Little Tennessee, Hiwassee, and Tellico Rivers and the Cheowa River in western North Carolina. The Otali dialect or Western dialect was spoken in the Upper Towns.

The Cherokee national government was effective and divided into two organizations, one addressing peace and the other war. Chosen headmen

Cherokee Micah Swimmer sharing his culture during Cherokee Heritage Days at Sycamore Shoals. *Courtesy of Michael Byerley.*

from each town made up the Tribal Council, and the women chose a leader for the National Women's Council, who was referred to as the Ghighau, meaning "most honored/beloved woman." Nancy Ward was the last woman to hold this office of honor. When her first husband, Kingfisher, was killed at the Battle of Muskogee in 1755, Nancy grabbed his rifle and fought alongside the other warriors. This heroic act resulted in her having the role of Ghighau bestowed on her.[18]

The Cherokee Mother Town of Kituwah is the Cherokee place of origin, the first village established by people who later became Cherokee. It is upheld and supported by the three federally recognized Cherokee tribes, which focus on their culture, political decisions, economic development, legal protection of tribal sovereignty and rights, community interactions, and education. Kituwah has been dated to ten thousand years ago using archaeological evidence. Located on the Tuckasegee River, it is one of the seven Cherokee mother towns and is located nine miles from the town of Cherokee.[19]

The village of Kituwah was burned in 1761 by Colonel James Grant's forces, though people continued to live there after the attack. In 1776, General Griffith Rutherford and Colonel William Christian planned to attack the Cherokee towns in retaliation for Cherokee attacks on frontier settlements in the Watauga, Nolichucky, and Holston settlements of today's northeast Tennessee and settlements in North and South Carolina.

Rutherford's Light Horse expedition from October 17 to November 16, 1776, against the Lower, Middle, and Overhill Cherokee towns again destroyed the town of Kituwah.

Years prior to this event, the British and their Indian agents Alexander Cameron and James Stuart were arming the Cherokee to fight against the settlers west of the mountains, in hopes they would return to the colonies and into the control of King George III. The Cherokee warriors, led by Dragging Canoe and his Chickamaugans, were fighting to keep and regain lands that had been traded by the elder chiefs to the never-ending westward flow of white settlers.[20]

Prior to 1700, early British traders, such as Needham and Arthur, interacted with the Cherokee people in their towns. Sir Alexander Cumming arrived in Charleston, South Carolina on December 5, 1729, and toured the American backcountry into early 1730. To avert war with the Cherokee, he encouraged Attakullakulla and six other Cherokee to visit London with him and meet King George II; they arrived in England on June 5, 1730. After much fanfare and discussion, they signed the Articles of Friendship and Commerce on September 9, 1730, which recognized the Cherokee as subjects of the Crown. The treaty provided for trade, made some Cherokee land available to British settlers, guaranteed the return of enslaved people held by the Cherokee in exchange for guns, and ensured the Cherokee would fight against any group that threatened the British. This treaty remained in effect for approximately thirty years.

The Cherokee then returned to South Carolina, arriving on February 18, 1731, while Cumming remained in London. It was discovered he had planned to defraud the Charleston colonists and was subsequently sent to Fleet Prison.

The journal of Lieutenant Henry Timberlake is considered a primary written source that shares the customs, dress, lifeways, and Cherokee history he observed. Timberlake was born in Virginia in 1730 and was, by profession, a colonial journalist and cartographer. After joining the Virginia military as a British officer in 1756, he served during the French and Indian War and was assigned in 1761 to the command of Colonel Adam Stephen. His regiment was involved in building a 120-foot log fort with four bastions, named Fort Robinson, in present-day Kingsport, Tennessee. Stephen's intent was to "have a post maintained here, either by the King or Colony." During this time, a large group of Cherokee arrived. Chief Kanagatucko (Old Hop) appealed for peace, which was granted to him on November 19, 1761, by Colonel Stephen, who had previously intended to retaliate against the Cherokee for the August 1760 attack on Fort Loudoun. The chief then asked for an officer to travel to Cherokee lands to prove that the war was over.

Timberlake volunteered to go with Kanagatucko to the Cherokee villages on the Little Tennessee river. Following four hundred returning Cherokee warriors, he carried with him the Treaty of Long Island of the Holston. He traveled with four others: Sergeant Thomas Sumter, who funded the journey, John McCormack, an interpreter, and a servant. On his arrival, he was greeted by the head man of Tomotley, Chief Ostenaco. Timberlake explained the peace treaty to the Cherokee people, offering assurances that it would be honored.

Timberlake's efforts were successful. After two years of violent conflict, a treaty arose because of the truce between the Cherokee and Colonel Stephen. An important component of the treaty prevented retaliation by Stephen for the Cherokee siege of Fort Loudoun, which ended with the surrender of the fort on August 8, 1760.

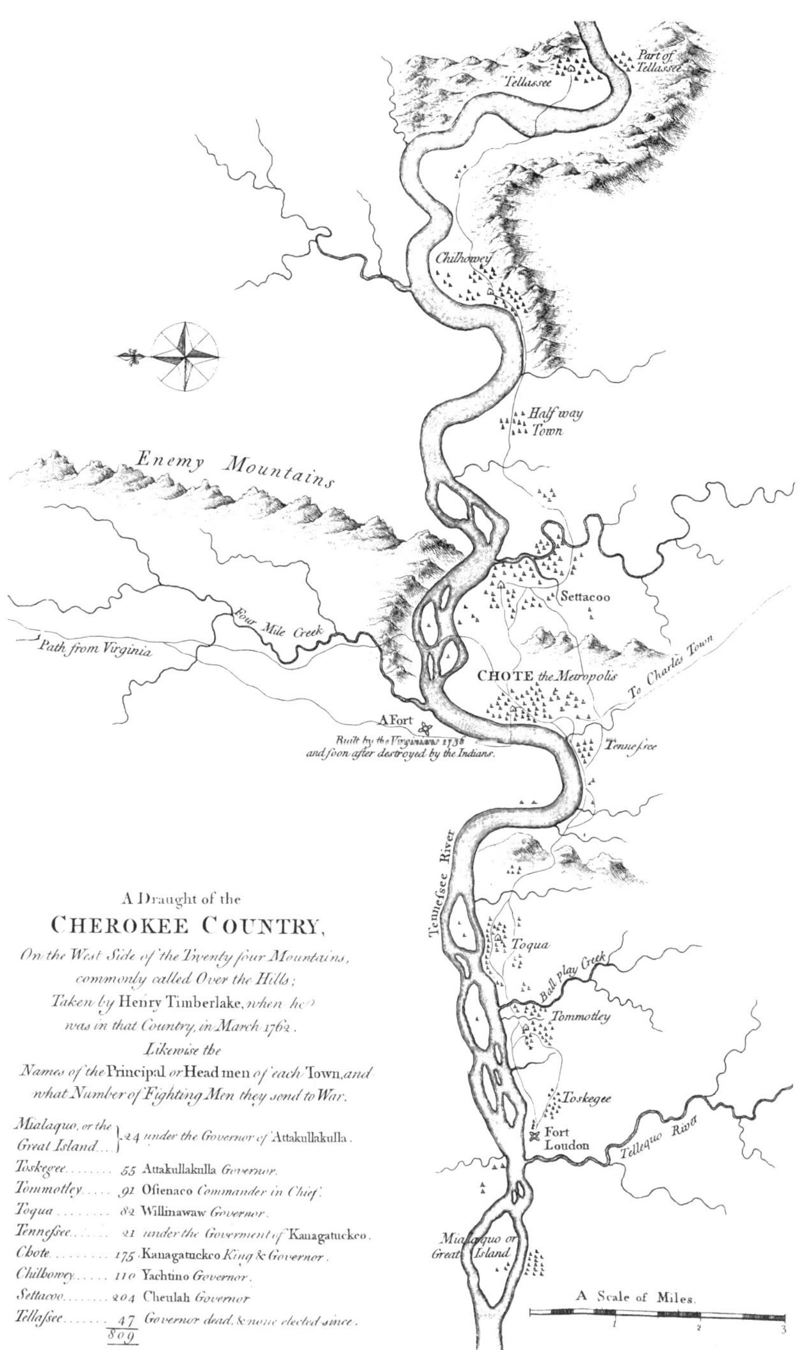

Henry Timberlake's map, "A Draught of the Tennessee Country," March 1762. *Courtesy Tennessee State Library and Archives.*

Lieutenant Henry Timberlake escorts three Cherokee chiefs to London in 1762 to meet King George III. *Courtesy of Sycamore Shoals State Historic Park.*

By early 1762, Chief Ostenaco, concerned about skirmishes taking place between white settlers and rival northern tribes, requested that Timberlake escort him, along with several hundred warriors, to Williamsburg to ensure peace. While in Williamsburg, Ostenaco asked Timberlake to take him to London to meet King George III. Hence, in May 1762, Cherokee Chiefs Ostenaco, Cunne Shote, and one other sailed to London to meet the king of England, making this the second time in world history that European royalty met with Native Americans. By August 25, 1762, the Cherokee were back in America.

In the summer of 1764, five Cherokee asked Timberlake to take them to see the Virginia governor, hoping they would be given passage back to London. Their goal was to encourage King George III to enforce the Proclamation Line of 1763. After the governor of Virginia denied their request for financial help, Timberlake decided he would find a financier. Unexpectedly, the financier of the trip died not long after the Cherokee's arrival in London. On top of that, Lord Halifax would not grant an audience with the king as the Cherokee visit was not authorized. The British government returned the

Cherokee to North America in March, while Timberlake, who remained in England, was accused of trying to make money off the Cherokee's presence. As he did not have the funds to pay their lodging bills, Timberlake was put in debtor's prison, where he died in 1765.

Timberlake's most noteworthy accomplishment was his journal, which he kept while living with the Cherokee. He was one of the first people to document Cherokee life and culture prior to European contact from the perspective of an Englishman. He recorded their customs, religious beliefs, agriculture, society, political structure, landholdings, and reactions to European colonists, along with other details. While living with them, he took a Cherokee wife: Ostenaco's daughter, Sakinney. Ostenaco lived with his grandson, Richard Timberlake, in his later years.

Timberlake's journal, currently published as *The Memoirs of Lieutenant Henry Timberlake*, was first published in London in 1765, the year of his death. It is assumed that he wrote his memoirs during his imprisonment. Timberlake's journal has been published several times; the most current edition, from 2007, was edited by Duane H. King and the Museum of the Cherokee Indian Press.

Amid the changes occurring around the Cherokee people during the eighteenth century, the British efforts focused on colonizing America presented a myriad of challenges. Native tribes continued to maintain their traditional way of life, including hunting, gathering, and farming, while some adopted the lifestyle of the colonists. The foreign diseases they were exposed to, and to which they were not immune, were devastating and significantly reduced their numbers.

By the early part of the eighteenth century, the Cherokee and Chickasaw had chosen to engage in both military and trading alliances with the British. Several Iroquoian tribes, traditional enemies of the Cherokee, became allies with the French. The tribes that were in the Southeast became referred to as the five civilized tribes: the Cherokee, Creek, Choctaw, Chickasaw, and Seminole.

As allies, Native people traded pelts, furs, and other goods with settlers in exchange for European weapons and tools—which, in turn, were often used to conduct warfare due to loss of Native lands and the growing number of colonists. One early example of trade with settlers is seen in early Woodland bison powder horns that have survived. By 1883, less than twenty-five thousand bison remained due to commercial hunting, diseases from domestic cattle, degradation of habitat, and railroad expansion, all of which moved them close to extinction.[21]

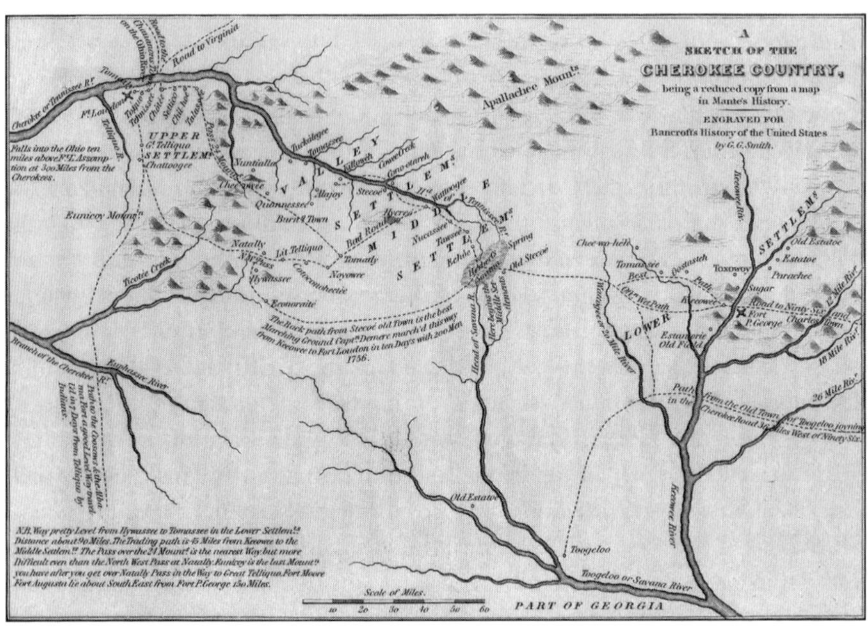

A sketch of the Cherokee towns in 1772 by G.G. Smith. *Courtesy of the Tennessee State Library and Archives.*

After the United States became an independent nation, new treaties were written related to the Native people of America. They had already engaged with and signed a number of treaties with European colonists prior to American independence from Great Britain, prior to the French and Indian War, into the American Revolution, and through the War of 1812.

The Treaty of 1817 with the Cherokee Nation set the stage for what later became the forced removal of the Cherokee from their ancestral lands. This treaty forced them to cede their land to the United States government in exchange for land in a designated reservation area in Oklahoma; annual payments were made to compensate for relinquished lands. After the passage of this treaty, a group of Cherokee known as the Old Settlers chose to move west. The people of the town of Kituwah exchanged their land in the Southeast and settled in present-day Arkansas long before the forced removal of 1838. After eleven years in Arkansas, they relocated to Oklahoma and became recognized as the United Keetoowah Band of the Cherokee.

In 1819, the Civilization Fund Act was created to deal with what was called the "Indian problem." The act encouraged nonprofit organizations and charitable groups to provide education for Native people and provided an annuity to stimulate the "civilization process." Teaching Native people to

Sequoyah is known for his development of a writing system for the Cherokee language called the Cherokee syllabary. *Courtesy of the Sequoyah Birthplace Museum.*

read and write in the English language was followed by attempting to make them give up their native culture, language, and religious practices. This was presented as "civilized" behavior.

The 1819 act was followed in 1824 by the creation of the Bureau of Indian Affairs, which ultimately resulted in the loss of land for the Cherokee people and other tribal nations. Just eleven years later, the Indian Removal Act of

1830 was enacted by President Andrew Jackson. The act attempted to move all Native nations in the southern United States to present-day Oklahoma, then called Indian Territory. The case was taken to the Supreme Court, where it was determined that removal was unconstitutional. The removal moved forward regardless.

Prior to removal, Sequoyah saw the need for developing a writing system for the Cherokee language. His exposure to written communication between Europeans inspired him to create a writing system that supported the sounds of his own language; each symbol represented a syllable, rather than using an alphabet. He completed it by 1821 and called it the Cherokee syllabary. At a very volatile time, when their civilization and lands were being challenged, the Cherokee people were now able to record their history in writing and learned to read through this new method of communication. This great accomplishment provided a pathway that enhanced preservation of Cherokee language and traditions, along with learning, literacy, and a bilingual newspaper, the *Cherokee Phoenix*.

The Sequoyah Birthplace Museum, located on Tellico Lake in Vonore, Tennessee, has served as an educational site since 1986, telling the story of the Cherokee with a special emphasis on the accomplishments and contributions of Sequoyah to the Cherokee people. Sequoyah is honored by his people for his development of the Cherokee syllabary and the new opportunities it provided.

After Cherokee removal from their eastern homeland to Oklahoma in 1838 and 1839 on what is referred to by the Cherokee people as the Trail of Tears Where They Cried, it is estimated that one-fourth to one-half of the Cherokee population perished by the end of their first year in Oklahoma. Over three hundred Cherokee found ways to remain; they were federally recognized as the Eastern Band of the Cherokee in 1868. During the removal, Kituwah moved out of their control and was later used for crops and as a grass landing strip. In 1996, the Eastern Band of the Cherokee Indians bought 309 acres of Kituwah, including the mound; this land went into a trust in 2021.

Today, there are three federally recognized Cherokee tribal nations: the Eastern Band of Cherokee Indians, the Cherokee Nation, and the United Keetoowah Band, all of whom operate their own governments and are considered sovereign nations. The Eastern Band are those who found ways to stay in their ancestral homelands during the removal in 1838. Later, they were able to buy back land in what is now the Qualla Boundary in Cherokee, Graham, Haywood, Jackson and Swain Counties in North

Carolina. Tahlequah, Oklahoma, is the capital of the Cherokee Nation and the United Keetoowah Band of Cherokee, though members live in other states.

In 1990, the Native American Graves Protection and Repatriation Act (NAGPRA) was passed by the United States Congress. This important legislation provides for the protection of human remains and objects of Native people and their culture. Unethical collecting and object theft related to looting can now be addressed through legal means. The law also provides Native nations with a legal option to seek repatriation of their ancestral human remains and cultural objects. NAGPRA applies only to federal lands and federally funded institutions and does not address the entire issue of unethical collection of Native peoples' ancestral human remains and cultural objects.

The Museum of the Cherokee People, a nonprofit 501(c)(3) organization, was established in 1948 on ancestral homelands of the Cherokee in Cherokee, North Carolina. It is one of the longest-operating tribal museums in the country and presents engaging exhibits, demonstrations, and educational programs; historical research; and a host of opportunities for the public to learn about Cherokee culture.

The Oconaluftee Indian Village in Cherokee, North Carolina, shares Cherokee history, culture, and lifeways from the eighteenth century through today. The outdoor drama *Unto These Hills*, which celebrated seventy-five years in 2025, tells the stories of the Cherokee people beginning with first European contact in the 1540s through their forced removal on the Trail of Tears.

Of all the sovereign Cherokee nations, the Cherokee Nation in northeastern Oklahoma and headquartered in Tahlequah is the largest tribe in the United States. The United Keetoowah Band is also in Oklahoma and headquartered in Tahlequah. They are also known as the Western Cherokee, or Old Settlers. In Cherokee, North Carolina, the Eastern Band of Cherokee Indians continues to preserve their history and share their stories within the fifty-seven thousand acres of the Qualla Boundary in western North Carolina.

Chapter 3

SETTLING THE RIVERS

The Watauga, Nolichucky, and Holston

As the first settlers arrived in the Watauga River valley, they found the land was open with few trees and gave it the name Old Fields. As a great deal of nearby land was wilderness and forested, it raised the question of whether the Old Fields had been cleared and inhabited in the past by Native people.

N.E. Hyder, in 1903, described the location, writing that the Old Fields ran "from the mouth of Stony Creek, down (the Watauga) river to the mouth of Buffalo Creek at the bend of the river, about 8 miles." In Hyder's 1903 journal article "Watauga Old Fields," he says that the Cherokee chiefs were asked about them and responded, "They were always there." As families began the process of working the land, the Old Fields soon began to tell the stories of the lifeways of Indigenous people. Evidence was unveiled as stone tools, broken pottery, shell beads, arrow points, and other artifacts were discovered when land was tilled or disturbed.[22]

As more people moved west from the colonies, they came looking for land, freedom from British rule, and new opportunities. Families, longhunters, traders, and others came mostly from Virginia and its northern plantations and North Carolina, including the western mountains. Those who came from more well-to-do plantations brought their families, enslaved people, household items, personal belongings, livestock, and more, while others traveled with few possessions. By 1772, the Watauga settlement had seventy to eighty farms along the waterways, composed primarily of families from North Carolina and Virginia.

The Regulator Movement in North Carolina accounted for some of the families that moved to Watauga. They opposed the corrupt government that, they believed, implemented unfair taxes, and they were involved in altercations with the colonial government. In May 1771, the Battle of Alamance between the Regulators and Governor Tryon's army ended with the defeat of the Regulators. Soon after, many left their homes and moved west.

Traveling across the mountains offered a difficult trip at best, navigating thick vegetation, dense terrain, and often dangerous situations. Following early roads through Virginia was less treacherous. The Great Valley Road, which split from the Great Wagon Road at Roanoke, continued to Sapling Grove, now Bristol. It split in one direction toward Kentucky, taking on the name of the Wilderness Road, and in a second direction southeast, toward the Watauga settlement. In *Tennessee During the Revolutionary War*, Samuel Cole Williams describes the route to Watauga:

> *Passing down the Holston the route of travel divided after the site of Abingdon was passed. From there the main road traveled southwest to the Long Island of the Holston on the Island Road, built in 1761. A southward prong ran to the Watauga settlement through Shoate's Ford, today's Bluff City, which was laid out in 1773 and called "the Watauga Road."*

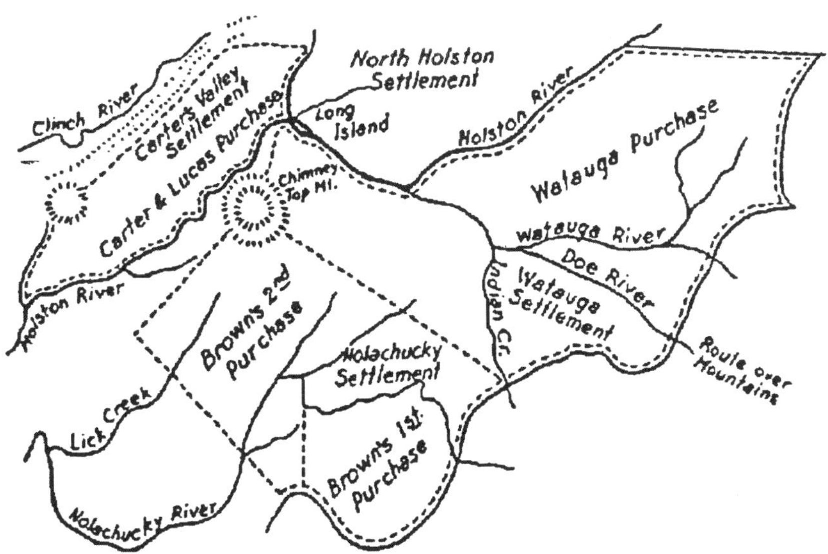

The first settlements near the Watauga, Nolichucky, and Holston Rivers. *Garrett and Goodpasture, 1900.*

Starting a new life on the frontier included making products needed for survival. This reenactor demonstrates how to make cordage, also called cord or twine. *Courtesy of the author.*

As settlers continued moving west, they often found themselves in places long inhabited by Native tribes, who, understandably, did not want the Europeans to settle on their lands. Their hope for a new start sometimes took a turn for the worse when the Indigenous people fought to keep their ancestral lands.

Our present knowledge of the names of those who arrived in the Watauga settlement, around the early 1770s onward, comes from well-referenced books, old letters, records of land transactions, military records, family stories and Bibles, signatures on treaties, pension records, and other government documents, which all aid in documenting people, events, and places in history.

The names of people we know today are many, but no doubt there are others of which records have not been found. The people who are named in this chapter, with selected information regarding their lives, represent a sampling of those from different walks of life who came to the Watauga, Nolichucky, and Holston settlements in the early 1770s. They are by no means the only people known to have been inhabitants of each settlement.

Many were involved politically and/or militarily, while others were inhabitants of a new community. Leaving the colonies, they were living on their own without protection from the colonial leaders and Great Britain. They found themselves on the frontier at a time when there were many challenges, some quite dangerous. Under strong leadership, they came together and formed growing settlements, nurtured military relationships with neighboring colonies, and fought for freedom from Great Britain during the Southern Campaign of the American Revolutionary War.

The settlers listed in the following pages represent many of those who are documented as having lived in the western settlements, beginning with those who were believed to be among the first settlers in the area of the Watauga Old Fields. Many bought and sold additional land and relocated within the Watauga, Nolichucky, and Holston settlements. As time passed, some moved even farther west as the settlements spread.

The First Known Settlers

William Bean, born around 1716, came from Pittsylvania County, Virginia, with his wife, Lydia, settling on Boones Creek in 1769. A farmer and a trader, he is often referred to as the first permanent settler in the Watauga settlement. Many of his relatives and neighbors from Pittsylvania County followed Bean and settled nearby, which gave Bean the significant title of colonizer. William and Lydia's first son, Russell, was the first child of European descent born west of the mountains.

John Honeycutt was possibly the second settler to locate upstream from William Bean. He built a "rude hut" near Roane Creek and the Watauga and visited there in 1770 with James Robertson, who later settled near Sycamore Shoals. In 1777, both John and James moved to the Holston River.

Andrew Greer, in 1766, was one of the first settlers and traders in the Old Fields, according to author James Gettys McGready Ramsey in his book *Annals of Tennessee*. Ramsey suggests that Greer built a hunting lodge for trading with the Natives before bringing his family. He registered his land in March 1775, at the mouth of Stoney Creek on the north bank of the Watauga, including Greer's Mill.

Joseph Greer, son of Andrew, born in 1760, fought at Kings Mountain. He is known for delivering the news of Ferguson's defeat at Kings Mountain to the Continental Congress. For his service in the fight for independence, Joseph received a land grant in today's Lincoln County, Tennessee, for three thousand acres. Later, in 1783, he bought Emanuel Carter's homeplace, in today's Elizabethton, from his widow, Sarah.

Julius Dugger settled at Dugger's Bridge, above today's Elizabethton. J.G.M. Ramsey believes Dugger was also a first settler and trader, arriving with Greer in 1766. Judge S.C. Williams and historians N.E. Hyder and Robert T. Nave all agree with Ramsey's assessment.

Daniel Boone, born in 1734 in Yadkin County, North Carolina, covered much ground in his days of exploring, hunting, and trading. He was best known for blazing a trail through the Cumberland Gap into Kentucky, opening a route for westward expansion.

Boone's whereabouts were often a mystery, but historians have found evidence of his travels over time. J.G.M. Ramsey writes that Boone traveled in 1761 from Wallen's Station with nineteen people, parting ways with them near today's Abingdon, Virginia. Ramsey also believed that Boone hunted in Watauga.

S.C. Williams states that Boone was a neighbor of James Robertson around 1772. Boone reportedly had a hunting camp nearby. A daughter of James's wife, Charlotte, recalled her mother saying, "Boone's children along with her own were christened in the Robertson home by a minister passing through the region."[23]

Opposite: Travel on horseback was common for hunting parties and military groups along with those looking for new places to settle. *Courtesy of Steve Ricker.*

Left: Spinning thread from flax, cotton, and wool to make thread or yarn, which was then woven into cloth to make clothing and other needed items. *Courtesy of Sycamore Shoals State Historic Park.*

When Ramsey was writing his 1853 book *Annals of Tennessee*, he received an inscription from N. Gammon of Jonesborough copied from a beech tree near Boone's Creek, saying, "D. Boon CillED A. BAR oN ThE Tree in yEAR 1760." If Boone, in fact, carved these words, he would have been twenty-six years old at the time. Whatever the case may be, Boone was often on the move and was said to be at his finest when in solitude with nature.

LIVING IN THE WATAUGA SETTLEMENTS NEAR THE WATAUGA AND HOLSTON RIVERS

Locations of settlers' homeplaces are given, if known.

GENERAL JAMES ROBERTSON, born in 1742 in Brunswick County, Virginia, later moved to Orange and then Wake County, North Carolina. The Regulation Movement was in full swing when Robertson decided to visit Watauga around 1770. He must have been impressed, as he called it the Promised Land.[24]

In his book *The Wataugans*, Max Dixon describes Robertson planting a crop of corn and building a corncrib and a cabin before he "headed back east in August—getting lost on the way. For two weeks he tried to find a different way home across the mountains." He climbed trees looking for something familiar, cut bushes to mark his course, and found he sometimes crossed his previous tracks. He was on the verge of starvation, and his gunpowder became too wet to spark, so he couldn't kill game. Just when he thought he could not go any farther, he ran into two hunters who fed him and helped him find his way home.[25]

Robertson returned to Watauga in September, accompanied by his wife, Charlotte Reeves, and their one-year-old child, along with family members: his sister Ann, William Reeves, and perhaps others. Estimates of the size of their party vary; it may have been as large as eighty people. On arrival, they settled in the vicinity of Sycamore Shoals. Some references indicate that Robertson lived at some point near Daniel Boone, who was closer to William Bean. S.C. Williams reports that Robertson planted his first crop and built a cabin near the junction of the Doe and Watauga Rivers.[26]

James did not hesitate to take on leadership roles in the settlement in political and military affairs. His name is associated with many of the important accomplishments of the Wataugans.

Children on the frontier always found time for play along with their daily chores. *Courtesy of Sycamore Shoals State Historic Park.*

In 1779, James, along with JOHN DONELSON, traveled to the Cumberland River, Robertson by land and Donelson by water. Together, they founded Fort Nashborough at present-day Nashville. In 1780, James drew up the Cumberland Compact, a constitution that many felt was written in the same manner as the Watauga Association Compact.

James later became a brigadier general in 1790, when the Southwest Territory was formed; a member of the North Carolina Legislature in 1796; and a member of the constitutional convention that framed Tennessee's first constitution. His many accomplishments earned him the title, Father of Middle Tennessee.

COLONEL JOHN DONELSON was a frontiersman, politician, explorer, surveyor, and ironmaster who moved to Watauga in the 1770s. He surveyed the new Cherokee boundary line in 1777 and attended the signing of the Treaty of Long Island at Fort Patrick Henry. Donelson left the Holston River area in the winter of 1779–80 and took a flotilla of settlers to present-day Nashville to meet Captain James Robertson, who traveled by land. Winter weather and attacks by Natives slowed the progress of the flotilla, along with losses, which included James's son John.

Together, Donelson and Robertson founded the first settlement at that location in 1780, named Fort Nashborough after General Francis Nash. The Creek and Chickamauga Cherokee launched repeated attacks against the settlements for many years.

In 1786, Governor of the State of Franklin JOHN SEVIER related the severity of the situation in a letter to Governor Telfair of Georgia: "Hostilities [by native tribes] are daily committed in the vicinities of Kentucky and Cumberland. Colonels Donelson, Christian, and several other persons, were lately wounded and are since dead." John Donelson died on November 17, 1785.

Attacks and retaliation continued until the death of Cherokee war chief DRAGGING CANOE on February 29, 1792. Though some attacks continued for a short time thereafter, Dragging Canoe's death marked the end of the resistance.

Surveyor WILLIAM BAILY SMITH played a part in marking roads and the boundaries of ever-increasing land claims. In 1775, Smith was living on the Watauga, and later that year, he moved to Kentucky to enter the service of Richard Henderson after the Transylvania land purchases. The same year, James Smith purchased his surveying equipment.

Surveyor JAMES SMITH was charged with surveying many of the early Watauga land warrants and was later credited with running the line between Washington and Sullivan Counties in 1788.

Living on the North Side of the Watauga River

Valentine Sevier Sr., born in London, became a miller and merchant while living in Virginia. He settled on the Holston in 1773, close to his son John's property. On December 28, 1778, he claimed acreage along the Watauga. On the same date, his son Colonel Valentine Sevier Jr. entered his land grant, where the "Sycamore Shoals extend along its banks." Their land grants state that they were the first landowners in the Old Fields. Valentine Sevier Sr. built a fort upriver from the Watauga Fort after it was attacked.

Valentine Sevier Jr. was active in the military while at Watauga. He moved to middle Tennessee in 1789, where he built a stone house and Sevier's Station, a small frontier outpost, on 640 acres from a Revolutionary War land grant. Three years later, his outpost was attacked, and three of his sons were killed by Natives. In 1794, he lost two daughters, one of their husbands, two grandchildren, and his six-year-old son when Sevier's Station was attacked by approximately forty Natives. The station is the oldest standing structure in Montgomery County, Tennessee.

Jeremiah Dungan built a stone manor and mill in 1778 in today's town of Watauga. His family worked the mill until 1866, when it was sold to George W. St. John. In 1996, it was honored as the state's oldest business, having operated continuously for over two hundred years.

Jacob Chamberlain settled on the north side of the Watauga, bordering Joshua Houghton Sr. and Valentine Sevier Sr.

Others living on the north side of the Watauga were Joseph and John Duncan and George Russell.

Godfrey Carriger Sr. was the first settler on Stoney Creek at Carriger's Landing, where it empties into the Watauga River. Corn, wheat, wrought iron, and other products were loaded onto flatboats there. His son Christian built a brick house nearby.

Drury Goodwin became the first landowner on the east side of Stoney Creek in May 1779, when his land warrant was issued.

Living on the South Side of the Watauga River at Sycamore Shoals

Colonel John Carter, born around 1737 in Virginia, married Elizabeth Taylor around 1758 and had three known sons, Landon, John Jr., and Emanuel. John Jr. and Emanuel owned land adjoining their father's property. Samuel Cole Williams writes of John as a merchandiser in the firm of Carter and Trent in northern Virginia. Near 1770, Carter and William Parker set up a trading post in Carter's Valley near the Holston River. After trading disagreements with the Cherokee, the store was robbed. Sometime later, Carter moved to the Watauga settlement and built a home on the south side of the Watauga River, now called the Carter Mansion. John was one of the settlement's strongest leaders up until his death in 1780, serving as chairman of the Watauga Association's first Committee of Five, the wartime Committee of Safety, and the Washington County court, along with holding many other leadership roles.[27]

Captain Landon Carter, son of John Carter, was born in 1760. In 1784, he married Elizabeth Maclin, the daughter of William and Sarah Maclin. During the American Revolution, he served under Colonel John Sevier and Colonel Arthur Campbell. Among his many accomplishments, he was educated at Liberty Hall, North Carolina; signed the Watauga Petition; participated in the battle of Boyd's Creek against the Cherokee; and strongly supported the State of Franklin. His leadership earned him the honor of later having Carter County named for him when the county was created and Elizabethton named for his wife after Tennessee became a state.

After the Carter's Valley trading post was robbed, William Parker possibly returned to Virginia and served in the Revolution as a lieutenant. He later resided near John Carter. After his death, Joseph Greer raised his children.[28]

William Tatham was born in 1752 in Cumberland County, England. In Virginia, he gained employment with the mercantile house of Carter and Trent on the James River. In *William Tatham and the Culture of Tobacco* by G. Melvin Herndon, Herndon writes about Tatham going back to Virginia in the fall of 1777 and returning in the spring of 1780 to again work for John Carter.[29] William authored the Watauga Petition to the North Carolina Assembly and tutored Landon Carter.

Tatham was likely considered an asset based on his experience and intelligence; he worked as a clerk, surveyor, soldier, lawyer, merchant, geographer, mapmaker, and more. He possibly learned surveying and engineering from William Bailey Smith.

Tatham, along with Colonel John Todd, wrote *History of the Western Country*, with the goal of providing a detailed history of the Watauga settlement. It was reviewed by Tatham's close acquaintance Thomas Jefferson,

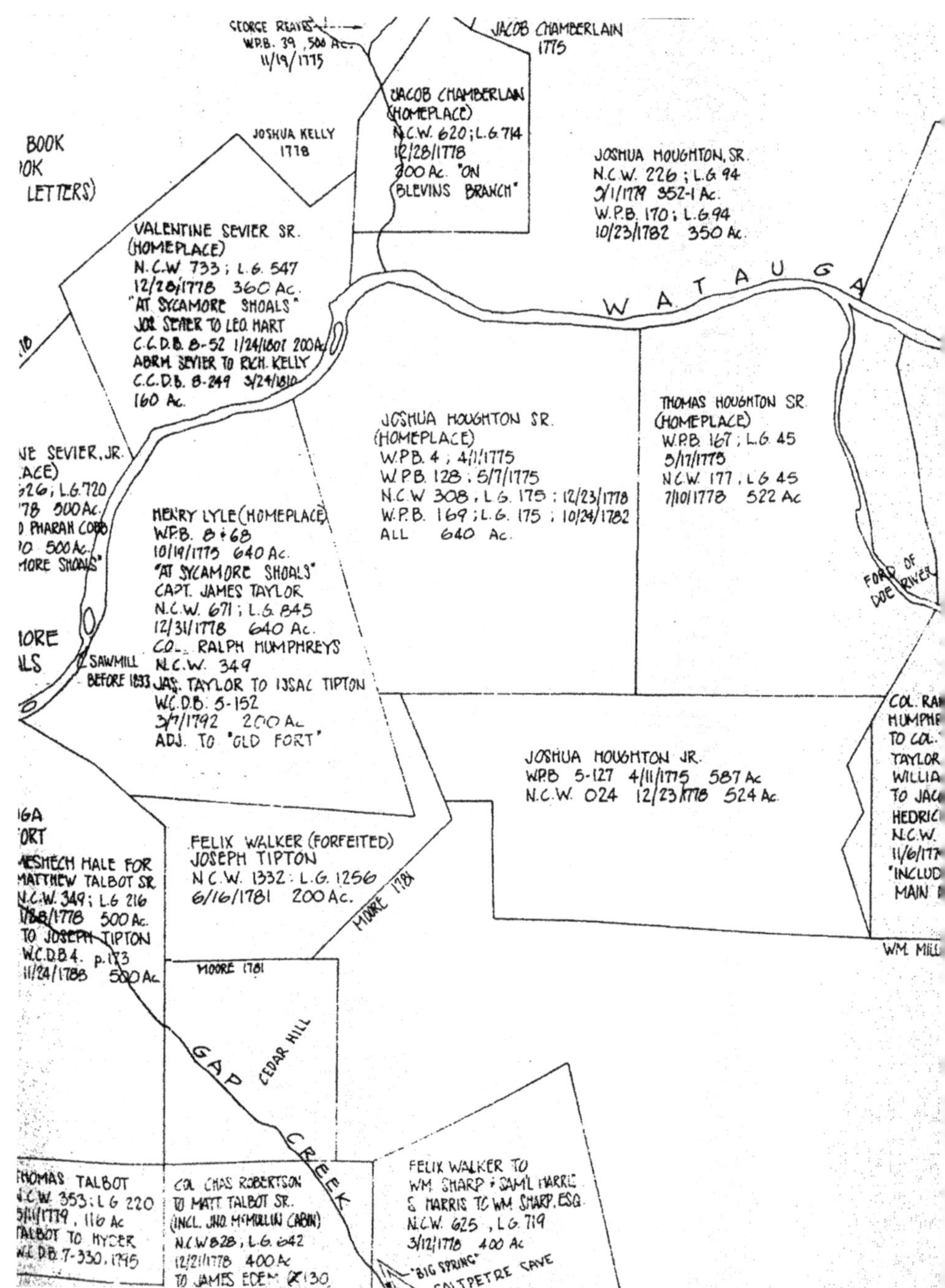

This two-page map shows some of the first landowners to register their land in 1775 along the Wataugа River. *Courtesy of Sycamore Shoals State Historic Park.*

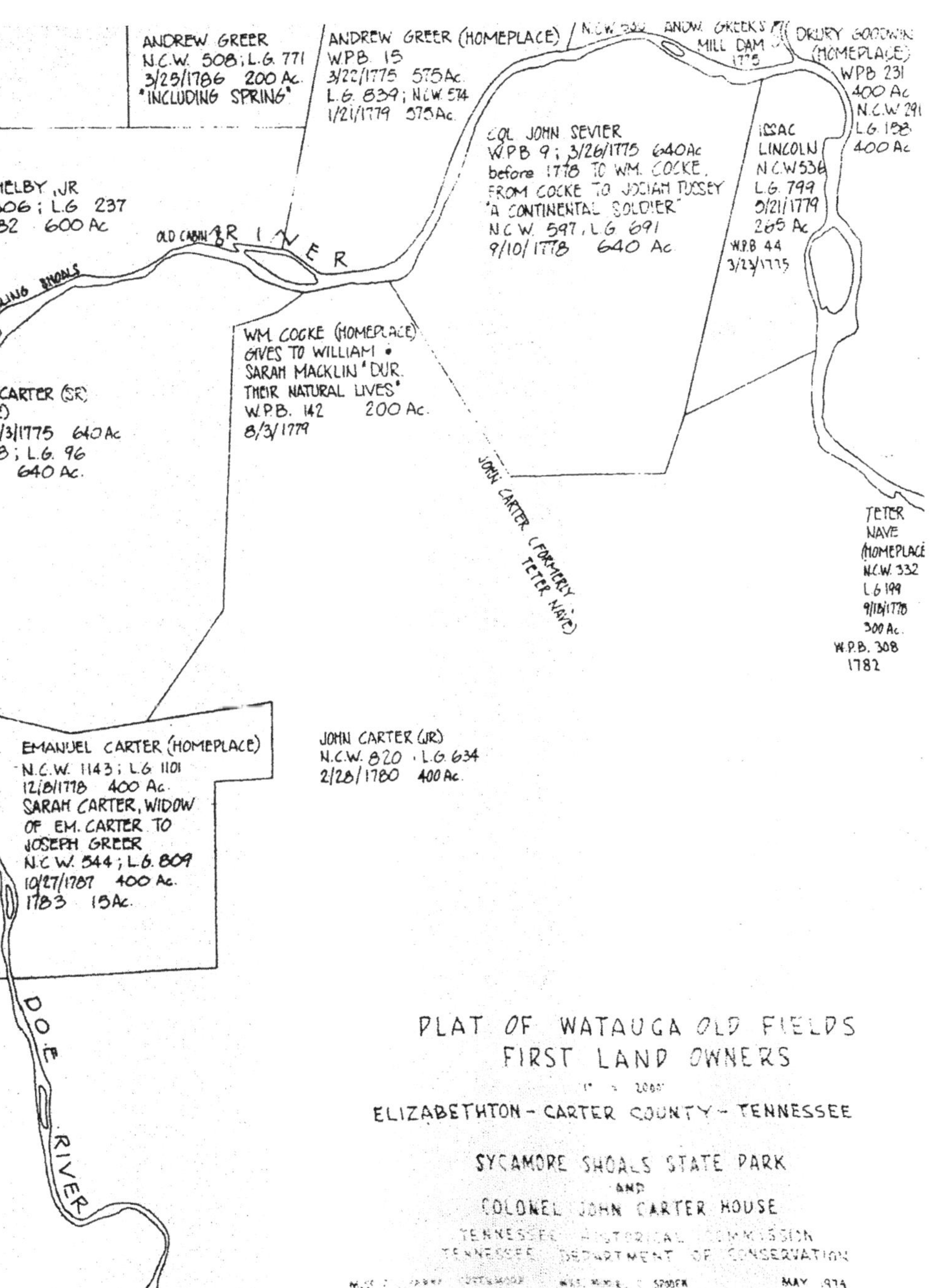
ANDREW GREER
N.C.W. 508; L.G. 771
3/25/1786 200 Ac.
"INCLUDING SPRING"
ANDREW GREER (HOMEPLACE)
W.P.B. 15
3/22/1775 575 Ac.
L.G. 839; N.C.W. 574
1/21/1779 575 Ac.
MILL DAM
DRURY GOODWIN
(HOMEPLACE)
WPB 231
400 Ac
COL JOHN SEVIER
W.P.B 9; 3/26/1775 640 Ac
before 1778 TO WM. COCKE.
FROM COCKE TO JOSIAH TUSSEY
"A CONTINENTAL SOLDIER"
N.C.W. 597, L.G. 691
9/10/1778 640 Ac.
ISSAC
LINCOLN
L.G. 799
5/21/1779
265 Ac
W.P.B 44
3/23/1775
OLD CABIN
RIVER
WM. COCKE (HOMEPLACE)
GIVES TO WILLIAM &
SARAH MACKLIN "DUR.
THEIR NATURAL LIVES"
W.P.B. 142 200 Ac.
8/3/1779
JOHN CARTER (FORMERLY TETER NAVE)
TETER
NAVE
(HOMEPLACE
N.C.W. 332
L.G. 199
300 Ac.
W.P.B. 308
1782
EMANUEL CARTER (HOMEPLACE)
N.C.W. 1143; L.G. 1101
12/8/1778 400 Ac.
SARAH CARTER, WIDOW
OF EM. CARTER TO
JOSEPH GREER
N.C.W. 544; L.G. 809
10/27/1787 400 Ac.
1783 15 Ac.
JOHN CARTER (JR)
N.C.W. 820 · L.G. 634
2/28/1780 400 Ac.
DOE RIVER
PLAT OF WATAUGA OLD FIELDS
FIRST LAND OWNERS
ELIZABETHTON - CARTER COUNTY - TENNESSEE
SYCAMORE SHOALS STATE PARK
AND
COLONEL JOHN CARTER HOUSE
TENNESSEE HISTORICAL COMMISSION
TENNESSEE DEPARTMENT OF CONSERVATION
MAY 1974

who, in commenting on Tatham and Todd's manuscript, said of Tatham, "He is particularly acquainted with the Western Country of Virginia and Carolina beyond the mountains of which he had made a pretty good map; he is versed in writing and accounts and possesses understanding." Sadly, the manuscript was lost while he was serving as an officer under General George Washington during the Revolutionary War.[30]

General John Sevier, born in Virginia, moved to the Holston in late 1773. He first visited the settlements in 1771 and later in 1773, at a horse race in Watauga. A fellow named Shoate took a horse from a smaller man, saying he had won it on a bet. The owner denied Shoate's claim, and Sevier, bothered by this, concluded he could not settle in such a place.

Trying to calm him, Captain Shelby told Sevier, "Never mind those rascals; they'll soon take poplar [a canoe] and push off." Sometime after, Sevier learned that Shoate was apprehended and hanged as a horse thief. Later in 1776, after Colonel Christian's Cherokee campaign, Sevier moved to Watauga and lived upriver from John Carter. He served as the only governor of the State of Franklin and as the first and third governor of the state of Tennessee.

Catherine Sherrill was the daughter of Samuel Sherrill and became the second wife of John Sevier in 1780; she was later given the nickname Bonnie Kate. She was known for being able to outrun, outshoot, and outride any man in the settlement.

Major Valentine Sevier Jr., John's brother, settled near the upper end of Lynn Mountain.

Captain Robert Sevier was the son of Major Valentine Sevier Jr. He married Keziah Robertson, the daughter of Charles, and served in the battle at Kings Mountain. Robert died on his return home from wounds he received in battle.

Other settlers near Lynn Mountain include Josiah Tussey, Teeter Nave, and Isaac Lincoln, the great-uncle of President Abraham Lincoln whose land adjoined that of John Sevier.

Living closer to Sycamore Shoals on the south side of the Watauga were Henry Lyle, whose land adjoined Joshua Houghton Sr.; Joseph Tipton; and Meshech Hale. Thomas Houghton Sr. adjoined Joshua Houghton Sr., Joshua Houghton Jr., Colonel Ralph Humphries, and Colonel John Carter, mentioned above.

Colonel John Tipton first settled on the Watauga on the west side of the Doe River. After the Revolutionary War, he moved to today's Washington County, buying land in 1784 on Catbird Branch from Samuel Henry. There

A comfortable log cabin with a fireplace provided warmth and a wonderful place to cook. *Courtesy of the author.*

Preparing meals for the family began with growing food crops along with hunting for wild game. *Courtesy of the author.*

he built his home, now protected as Tipton Haynes State Historic Site. The Battle of the State of Franklin was fought in February 1788 at Tipton's home.

John Tipton Jr. moved to Watauga with his brother Joseph and his father, Colonel John Tipton, in the 1770s. He inherited his father's property, now Tipton-Haynes State Historic Site. After John Jr.'s death, the property was sold to David and Rhoda Haynes.

Robert Lucas, the son of Edward Lucas, lived on the north side of the Watauga River near a ridge aligned with the lower end of an island. Robert later moved to the Cumberland Settlement.

On the south side of Watauga, west of the Shoals, Arthur Cobb's homeplace bordered William McNabb and Cleavers Barksdell. Cobb's land went to his daughter Patience Cobb Cooper, wife of James Cooper, around 1775. The homeplace of William McNabb adjoined Charles Robertson, Arthur Cobb, and Cleavers Barksdell.

William Cocke settled between Colonels John Carter Sr. and John Sevier. Cocke later gave his land to William Maclin and wife, Sarah, who were the parents of Elizabeth Maclin, who married Landon Carter.

Others living on the south side of the Watauga were Felix Walker, Teter Nave, John Jones, and Isham Yirby.

LIVING ON BUFFALO, SINKING, AND GAP CREEKS

SIMEON BUNDY was the first settler on Gap Creek near Big Spring. Within two years, his acreage was transferred to MATTHEW TALBOTT SR.

JAMES EDENS, THOMAS GOURLEY, WILLIAM BOYD, and JOSEPH RYDER all lived near Big Springs on Gap Creek near SIMEON BUNDY.

COLONEL CHARLES ROBERTSON settled on Buffalo and Sinking Creek by 1772 with his wife, SUSANNAH NICKOLS, on land adjoining JONATHAN TIPTON, CHRISTOPHER CUNNINGHAM, and ROBERT YOUNG. His daughter KEZIAH ROBERTSON married ROBERT SEVIER. Lyman Draper, corresponding with the Robertson family, determined that this Charles was the cousin of JAMES ROBERTSON.

Charles was one of the five judges of the Watauga Court with the first court held at his Sinking Creek home. Other courts met at the home of MATTHEW TALBOTT. When the Cherokee sold the Watauga settlers their land via The Watauga Purchase deed of March 19, 1775, the deed gave Charles ownership of all lands, which he in turn sold to the settlers. He became the first trustee of the Watauga Association, recording land transactions in what was later called Deed Book A.

Lyman Draper, an educator and historian, in describing Charles Robertson, wrote, "He was distinguished for his great good sense and wisdom, not less than his virtue." Draper is best known for the Draper Manuscript Collection, which covers the period between the French and Indian War and the War of 1812.

MATTHEW TALBOT SR., a Baptist minister from Virginia, arrived by 1775. He was preaching at Sinking Creek Baptist Church by 1776 and operated a gristmill on Gap Creek. Matthew's old homeplace was between the mouths of Buffalo and Gap Creeks; it was later owned by JOSEPH TIPTON SR., who sold 361 acres to BRIGADIER GENERAL NATHANIEL TAYLOR in May 1809 on property that the main wagon road crossed. Matthew's sons—MATTHEW JR., JAMES, and THOMAS—all served in the battle of Kings Mountain. MATTHEW SR. later became the governor of Georgia.

CAPTAIN JOHN SHELBY SR. settled along Gap Creek and built Shelby's Station, a fort and trading post near the Holston. Shelby served in the Battle of Kings Mountain along with six other Shelby family members.

JOHN SHELBY JR. settled on Gap Creek on the south bank of the Watauga, opposite the Tumbling Shoals, with his father, CAPTAIN JOHN SHELBY SR. Later, he operated Shelby's Station, his father's trading post north of the Holston.

The younger gentlemen of a settlement enjoyed social time with friends and games of all kinds. *Courtesy of Sycamore Shoals State Historic Park.*

Andrew Taylor Sr., the father of Brigadier General Nathaniel Taylor, had a 450-acre land grant adjoining Cleavers Barksdell and Matthew Talbott. Andrew built a mill on a branch of Buffalo Creek.

Robert Young's tract was "under the foot of Buffalo Mountain." He served at Kings Mountain and was credited with firing the shot that killed British Major Patrick Ferguson.

Mary McKeehan Patton married John Patton and moved to Powder Branch after the birth of their two children. Mary learned how to make gunpowder from her father, David McKeehan, and provided over five hundred pounds of powder to the Overmountain Men. She died on December 15, 1836.

Michael Hyder from Hampshire County, Virginia, arrived in 1772 and built a home and powder mill on Powder Branch, adjoining Andrew Taylor Sr.

John Williams lived on Gap Creek and was the brother of Jarrett Williams, the trader.

Mark Robertson, in 1775, claimed a 372-acre tract near Charles. He later joined his brother James on his journey to the Cumberland. In 1787, Mark was killed by Natives at Richland Creek.

Zachariah Isbell, from North Carolina, was an experienced magistrate and justice and a strong soldier. Later, he lived in Brown's settlement.

Baptist McNabb one of the earliest settlers, had settled near Samuel Henry Sr. on Buffalo Creek by 1778 at the latest. Ramsey stated that McNabb erected the first mill on Buffalo Creek. He lived near William McNabb and John McNabb. David McNabb married Elizabeth Taylor, daughter of Andrew Taylor.

Other names of those living on Gap, Buffalo, and Sinking Creeks include Cleavers Barksdell, Jessee Benton, Christopher Cunningham Sr., William Sharpe, the Moore family, James Denton (adjoining Joseph Tipton), Edmond Williams, Samuel Henry Sr., and Felix Walker.

Living in the Nolichucky Settlement

John Ryan was the first known settler in the Nolichucky Settlement and is presumed to be a Regulator from North Carolina.

Jacob Brown, born in 1736, was a trader from South Carolina and founded the Nolichucky settlement, where he owned a store and was a blacksmith. He purchased his claim in 1771.

John Hart settled on the Nolichucky River in the late 1770s.

Alexander Campbell, Abednego Inman, Abraham Rise, and Adam Wilson all lived on Big Limestone Creek.

Living Near the Holston River

Elisha Walling lived on the Holston, twelve miles above Knoxville, being the farthest settler to the west.

Captain Evan Shelby was born in Wales and settled in Pennsylvania and then Maryland before arriving near the Holston in late 1770. In 1772, he and his son Isaac had a store in Sapling Grove, which was frequented by many of the earlier settlers. His son John erected a station on the Holston. Sapling Grove was patented on June 20, 1753, by Colonel James Patton, which allowed him to sell tracts to settlers.

Shelby led a militia unit at the Battle of Point Pleasant during Lord Dunmore's War and served as a major in the Virginia militia and a colonel in the Washington District. When Washington County was formed, he served in the militia from 1776 to 1783.

Colonel Isaac Shelby, son of Evan Shelby, led a militia unit during the battle of Kings Mountain. He achieved the rank of major general during the War of 1812 and became the first governor of Kentucky.

Reverend Samuel Doak, as a young minister, was first sent to Washington County, near Abingdon, Virginia, on October 31, 1777. A year later, he moved to the Holston River to the Fork Church. He was the founder of Washington College Academy church and school, originally called Martin Academy. In 1780, as the Overmountain Men mustered at Sycamore Shoals, Doak delivered an inspirational prayer to the troops.

Jacob Womack was on the Holston near today's Bluff City by 1774–75. He built Womack's fort at his home and served at Kings Mountain under Colonel John Sevier.

Other settlers near the Holston included Edward Cox, who adjoined John Sevier; Gilbert Christian, near Long Island; Isaac Ruddle, near Ruddles Creek; Joseph Tipton, adjoining Edmund Roberts; Edward Lucas, above Jones's Great Falls; William Poage, near Long Island; William Blevins, above Long Island, adjoining John Cox Sr. and John Cox Jr.; Henry Grymes; and John Jones, who settled in the fork of Watauga and Holston.

ARCHIBALD TAYLOR lived west of today's Blountville near the first meetinghouse in 1772–73.

THOMAS SHOATE lived near today's Blountville.

RICHARD SHOATE lived near Hickory Creek in today's Sullivan County.

LIVING IN THE ROCKY MOUNT AREA

WILLIAM COBB and HENRY MASSENGILL SR. were early Watauga settlers, arriving at today's Rocky Mount around 1770. There, a two-story house was built of white oak logs, overlooking the Watauga River. Before the 1780 Kings Mountain muster at Sycamore Shoals, Cobb outfitted some of the frontiersmen en route to the rendezvous. In October 1790, this home served as a temporary capital of the Southwest Territory for about eighteen months. GOVERNOR WILLIAM BLOUNT, ANDREW JOHNSON, and DANIEL BOONE were all guests of the Cobbs.

The names of other Watauga settlers, whose locations are unconfirmed, include BENJAMIN PYBURN, ANDREWS LITTLE, JAMES HOLLIS, JOHN CASSADY, CHRISTOPHER SHOATE, THOMAS FARRER, JAMES ABBOT, JAMES WALDING, JOHN BEAN, THOMAS GRESHAM, AMBROSE HODGE, RICHARD BENNETT, RICHARD FLETCHER, GEORGE REEVES, SAMUEL DENTON, JAMES SMITH, ELIJAH ROBERTON (brother of James), GEORGE GRAY, CHARLES THOMPSON,

After a day's work, relaxing with a few tunes was always welcome. *Courtesy of Sycamore Shoals State Historic Park.*

JOHN CASSADY, THOMAS AMIS, DANIEL KENNEDY, JOHN COCKERILL, FELIX WALKER, and DAVID HUGHES.

We have taken but a mere glimpse into the names, places, and life experiences of a handful of the earliest travelers to the Watauga settlement. As you read on, you will recognize the names of several people introduced in this chapter and learn more about their contributions, challenges, and successes.

As word spread, each year saw larger numbers of people making their way to what would later become the Southwest Territory. Packing up all their possessions and their families and then journeying off into the unknown took a great deal of dedication and a strong belief that a better life lay ahead.

Chapter 4

THE WATAUGA ASSOCIATION, 1772

The Watauga Settlement has been described as the first American settlement located west of the Appalachian Mountains. Its inhabitants were primarily English, Highland Scot, and Scots-Irish immigrants. They moved west, leaving the British-controlled colonies, in search of land and freedom from British rule.

As settlers moving to Watauga continued to leave the colonies, confusion over land boundaries between themselves and the Cherokee became a never-ending issue. The confusion was understandable as boundary surveys and treaties associated with the Indigenous people were ever changing.

The Treaty of Paris of February 1763 not only officially ended the French and Indian War but also established the Mississippi River as a boundary between English and French land. That same year, the British king penned the Proclamation of October 1763 to prohibit settlements west of the eastern continental divide in order to keep the settlers in the colonies. It is probably not surprising that there were those who either knew nothing about it or ignored it, crossed the mountains, planted crops, and built a cabin. Albert Virgil Goodpasture, in *History of Tennessee*, points out that immigrants from the north used the lay of the land and waters to navigate, following rivers such as the Shenandoa and others. Frontiersmen looked at the Alleghany Mountains as the line between the British colonies and the lands of Native tribes. Yet settlements outside the colonies continued to grow as individuals and families from all walks of life moved down the valleys of southwest Virginia into the valleys of present-day east Tennessee.

The people of the Watauga settlement were mostly settlers of English, Highland Scot, and Scots-Irish descent. *Courtesy of Tim Massey.*

Five years later, in October 1768, the Treaty of Hard Labor ceded Cherokee lands west of the Allegheny Mountains and east of the Ohio River to the colonists. Then, in November 1768, the Treaty of Fort Stanwix, an agreement with the six nations of the Iroquois Confederacy, opened lands for settlement in the Northern Appalachians. These treaties moved the boundaries farther west, but the new boundaries were confusing.

To clarify the boundaries and to request additional land to accommodate the growing number of colonists, the Treaty of Lochaber was signed in October 1770. The gathering was held at Royal Indian Agent Alexander Cameron's Lochaber plantation in South Carolina and the treaty signed by Superintendent of Indian Affairs John Stuart. Its goal was to establish a clear western boundary of the frontier settlements of Virginia and North Carolina. Earlier boundaries were hard to identify and sometimes led people to believe they were legally within the boundaries of their colonies when, in fact, they were not.

In 1771, John Donelson surveyed the treaty line; the northern side of the line was at the mouth of the Kentucky River, west of the Kanawha River. By 1772, land in Virginia and eastern Kentucky had been ceded to the Colony of Virginia. At the same time, Virginia's southern boundary was established, located at the Holston River, which left only those north of the Holston under the protection of Virginia. Those living south of the Holston—in the Watauga, Nolichucky, and Carter's Valley settlements—were not in Virginia but on Cherokee land.

Soon after Donelson surveyed the new boundary line, Indian Agent Alexander Cameron warned the settlers in Watauga to move as they were illegally on Cherokee land and should abandon their landholdings.

After this unexpected turn of events, the settlers, who were unwilling to abandon their plantations and the work they had invested in their new homes, came together to meet and consider their options. Daniel Boone, who was living in Watauga at the time, advised that they stay, reportedly saying, "Now is the time to keep the country. If we give up now, it will never be the same." The settlers, who were in agreement, decided to ask for a delay to give them time to plan.[31]

The settlers asked the Cherokee if they could remain until their crops came in, which Cameron and the Cherokee accepted. The settlers used this extra time to devise a plan to form a government of their own and to deal with the Cherokee directly regarding their land. As they were forbidden by the Crown to buy land, they decided to ask the Cherokee for a lease.[32]

Indian Agent Alexander Cameron instructs the Watauga settlers to move as they are illegally on Cherokee land, so the settlers meet and plan to ask the Cherokee for a lease. *Courtesy of Sycamore Shoals State Historic Park.*

In the early spring of 1772, with self-government in the works, James Robertson and John Bean traveled to Chota to present their request. The Cherokee chiefs agreed to work with them and leased "all the country on the waters of Watauga" to them for ten years.[33] Indian Agent John Stuart approved the idea, but Alexander Cameron was completely opposed. Nonetheless, the lease was approved through Articles of Accommodation and Friendship in exchange for merchandise and trade goods valued at between $5,000 and $6,000 plus muskets and other household articles. Not long after, Jacob Brown negotiated a separate lease for the Nolichucky Valley land and then moved back to his store.[34]

Later, it was learned that many Cherokees protested this arrangement and believed that only a minority of their people were consulted. Learning that, possibly, only the Cherokee chiefs made the decision to give the Wataugans a ten-year lease without consulting others made it clear to the Watauga settlers that there was division within the Cherokee people. Many of the younger warriors, who did not want to lose ancestral lands, did not support the decisions of the older tribal members, who preferred negotiation and peace over war.

The requirements of the lease were not discussed until Little Carpenter traveled to Watauga to meet with the Watauga settlers. At this meeting, the settlers determined that for them to hold this lease, it was necessary to create a process to provide for negotiation among the settlers regarding land acquisition and distribution among them.

Thus, in the spring of 1772, after the lease was acquired, it became clear that some form of government was necessary to protect and organize the inhabitants of the Watauga Settlement. They were, for all intents and purposes, isolated from North Carolina and outside the boundary of Virginia. Moses Fisk, a nineteenth-century historian who was acquainted with James Robertson, wrote that those living in Watauga were "as little protected, controlled, or recollected by any government whatever, as their co-tenants the bears."[35]

The Watauga settlers came together under a sycamore tree to write and delineate the rules and regulations needed to fairly manage the affairs of the people. Adopting laws that mirrored those of Virginia, they wrote the Articles of the Watauga Association, their own constitution, which every member of the settlement was required to sign. They appointed five commissioners by majority vote, along with thirteen citizens to serve as commissioners.

There is no doubt that being told by the British to vacate their homes was a big concern for the Wataugans when negotiating their lease with

The settlers gathered to write and adopt the rules and regulations of the Watauga Association. *Courtesy of Sycamore Shoals State Historic Park.*

the Cherokee. Living on leased Cherokee land and not being under the protection of their neighboring colonies presented several important issues to be addressed. One of importance was the need to establish and uphold law and order on the frontier. The Articles of the Watauga Association called for a court to administer their new laws, to which five magistrates were elected, including a clerk and a sheriff. They did not want to become a "haven for those absconding debtors and fleeing felons who sought to put the high hills between themselves and their due."[36]

As the records of the association have been lost, it is uncertain who served as the first thirteen commissioners. Ramsey suggests they were John Carter, cousins Charles and James Robertson, Zachariah Isbell, John Sevier, James Smith, Jacob Brown, William Bean, John Jones, George Russell, Jacob Womack, Robert Lucas, and William Tatham.

Ramsey writes that John Carter served as chairman of the association and Charles Robertson, James Robertson, Zachariah Isbell, and John Sevier were selected to make up the court. According to Ramsey, William Tatham filled the role of clerk, though S.C. Williams believes James Smith was likely the first clerk and Valentine Sevier Jr. may have been the first sheriff. Williams also questions Sevier's involvement as he was on the Holston until at least 1775 and William Tatham did not arrive at Watauga until 1776. When

Sevier and Tatham arrived, they took on leadership roles in the association.[37]

Court sessions were to be held at the home of Charles Robertson but were also held at the home of Matthew Talbot between Gap and Buffalo Creek, south of the Watauga River.[38]

It did not take long before whispers of the Watauga Association's actions began to travel, and some were quite appalled. Virginia Governor Lord Dunmore, in 1774, referred to the Watauga Association as a "dangerous example" of Americans forming a government "distinct from and independent of his majesty's authority."

Virginia Governor Lord Dunmore felt the Watauga Association creating a new government was a "dangerous example." *Courtesy of Sycamore Shoals State Historic Park.*

For a time, life may have held a welcome peacefulness for the Watauga community. Improving their homesteads, tending to their families, growing crops, raising livestock, and trading with skilled craftsmen and others for metalwork, weaponry, gunpowder, and staples such as salt and cloth—all this is just a sampling of their needs on the frontier. With a sense of normalcy settling in and a lull in conflict, more hopeful settlers continued to move west.

Before long, the Cherokee, the Shawnee, and other native tribes held growing concerns about the number of white settlers moving farther and farther west onto their lands. Additionally, the Cherokee, unhappy with the Watauga lease, complained to Alexander Cameron about white encroachment, which affected their ability to hunt on their land due to settlement growth. Superintendent Stuart wrote to North Carolina Governor Martin, asking him to remove the western settlers. Governor Martin obliged, telling the Wataugans they should immediately vacate Indigenous territory—an order they ignored.

This order did concern the Watauga settlers, however, as the possibility of conflict existed, stemming from the killing of a Native named Billie. In 1774, while Billie was attending the horse races at Sycamore Shoals, he was shot by William Crabtree, who likely killed him in retaliation for the earlier killing of Crabtree's brother. The Natives at the horse races did not respond as they were unarmed and thus they returned quietly to their homes.

Worried that this event could cause a breakdown in relations with the Cherokee, James Robertson and William Faulin traveled to Chota to apologize and promised to arrest and punish Crabtree, which prevented a Cherokee attack.

AT THE START OF the American Revolution in 1775, the western settlements declared their independence from Great Britain. Together, they became the Washington District. Colonel John Carter served as chairman of the new Committee of Safety, which adhered to the Continental Congress and would be "indebted to the united colonies for their full proportion of the Continental expense."[39]

The accomplishments and growth of this fledgling government were impressive. Over a five-year period, the Watauga Association and its leaders found themselves transitioning from an independent government to being included in North Carolina as the Washington District, followed by Washington County, North Carolina. The leadership in place during these three changes in governmental organization held true to the association's beliefs and commitments to freedom and independence.

The Articles of the Watauga Association, a written compact for civil government, was the first such document west of the mountains.

The Watauga Association's written compact for civil government was the first west of the mountains. *Courtesy of Sycamore Shoals State Historic Park.*

Unfortunately, the original—or a copy of the document—has never been found, but there is always the possibility that additional information may come forth in the future.

There is a strong belief held by numerous historians and authors that the Articles of the Watauga Association were later used as a prototype for other similar resolutions on the ever-growing southwestern frontier. Some leaders present at Watauga were also present when similar documents were written in new frontier communities. The Boonesborough Resolutions of 1775 involved Richard Henderson and Daniel Boone, while the Cumberland Compact of 1780 included Richard Henderson and James Robertson. Documents governing the formation of the State of Franklin, under the leadership of John Sevier, were nearly identical to the Watauga articles, which may have been updated to reflect the needs of the time.

Historians consider the actions of the Watauga Association a highly significant event in the history of our nation. The establishment of self-government in a new land, on the western frontier, while under British rule has been considered by many historians a "milestone event" in American history.

In his book *The Wataugans*, author Max Dixon addresses this event in detail as interpreted by historians over time and presents "favorable observations." He notes that the native-born Americans penned the first constitution west of the Appalachian Mountains, along with, in the words of Lord Dunmore, "erecting themselves into a separate state…distinct from and independent of His Majesty's authority." The Watauga settlers asserted their independence and wrote a document providing rules and regulations for their community. In Dixon's words, the Articles of the Watauga Association were "one of the most thoroughly democratic instruments ever penned in the new world… absolutely free of religious tests and class distinctions" and the spontaneous action of a freedom-loving, "law-conscious band."[40]

Dixon also notes that some historians did not have "such an exalted view" of the Watauga Association:

> *Some historians, it is true, are less given to eulogizing hyperbole about democracy, freedom, and law consciousness; but the few if any would deny that the Watauga west was more free of political inequalities and class distinctions than Britain's seaboard colonies.*

A few historians have questioned the importance of the Wataugans' first constitution in the southwestern frontier, referring to it as a "squatters' agreement to create an organization simply to acquire land wholesale from the Indians and distribute it" and a "temporary expedient to meet a local security problem."[41] Dixon presents an interesting response:

> *Both of these charges might seem in some measure true, but two companion observations are in order. In weighing the significance of the Watauga Association, it would seem to matter very little that the constitution of this frontier community was tied to land questions and economic considerations—significant political movements and events tend regularly to have their origins in material interests. Similarly, the significance of an historical phenomenon is surely not lessened because it was undertaken to meet a crisis. This has often been the case in the history of revolution and change.*

President Theodore Roosevelt's three-part book *The Winning of the West*, published in 1889, 1894, and 1896, discusses the Watauga settlement on the western frontier, stating that the Watauga settlers were the "first men of American birth to establish a free and independent community on the continent."

With great determination, leadership, and a desire for a new life on a new continent, the citizens of the Watauga settlement came together in the spring of 1772 when they found themselves without protection from their neighboring colonies. They planned, organized, and implemented their own government on the frontier by adopting the laws of Virginia and adding local ordinances specific to their needs. They enforced their laws through their courts, raised and trained a militia, and negotiated with the Cherokee and British agents along with other colonial governments.

When the American Revolution began three years later, in 1775, the Watauga and Nolichucky settlements declared their independence from Great Britain. Just over four years after the Watauga Association was formed in 1772, on July 4, 1776, the Second Continental Congress approved the American Declaration of Independence, which was signed on August 2, 1776, at the Pennsylvania State House in Philadelphia.

In the same month, on August 22, the Watauga District's petition to the Provincial Council of North Carolina requesting annexation into North Carolina was received, "praying to be annexed to the province, in such a manner as might enable them to share in the glorious cause of liberty; enforce their laws under authority, and in every respect become the best members of society." In April 1777, the Watauga District became Washington County and the Wataugans citizens of the North Carolina colony.

Chapter 5

THE TREATY OF SYCAMORE SHOALS AND THE WATAUGA PURCHASE, 1775

Daniel Boone had long hoped to start a colony along the Kentucky River. In 1769, he began a two-year journey into Kentucky, around the same time that the Watauga settlement was in its infancy. He viewed land from Pilot Knob that appeared as a "magnificent forest enveloped in a blue haze but also a fabled garden interpenetrated with myth."[42]

Judge Richard Henderson of Hillsborough, North Carolina, also had interests in land speculation. After the French and Indian War, Boone assisted him in finding unsettled lands.

Of course, Boone was not the only person exploring Kentucky lands. Despite the continued fighting between Native tribes and settlers, many explorers were searching for new places to settle. On one occasion in 1773, Boone sent several members of his party back to Castlewood for supplies, including his son James and Henry Russell, son of William Russell. While they slept, their party was attacked by Shawnee, Delaware, and Cherokee warriors. James and Henry were brutally attacked and killed. Charles, one of the enslaved people with the group, was later found dead, along with their guide, Drake. Lord Dunmore, Virginia governor, ordered the punishment of those responsible, declared the Shawnee responsible, and urged the colonies to prepare for war.

In 1774, Colonel William Preston sent a surveying party to the Falls of the Ohio to claim that region. Dunmore also had plans to acquire land there for veterans from the French and Indian War. George Washington, who was also prospecting in the Ohio Valley, sent a surveyor to search for land "under the guise of hunting game."

Richard Henderson visited the Cherokee towns to propose his interest in buying Cherokee land in what is today's Kentucky. *Courtesy of Sycamore Shoals State Historic Park.*

Despite the loss of his son James in 1773, Boone's desire for a Kentucky colony never died, and his hopes rekindled after the 1774 defeat of the Shawnee in the Battle of Point Pleasant, a component of Lord Dunmore's War. After the Shawnee defeat, there was a sense that the Cherokee were concerned that their towns would become a target. This presented the possibility that they might sell a tract near the Kentucky River.

Driven by his strong interest in a Kentucky colony, Boone met with Richard Henderson, whose term as judge had ended, to suggest that he and other North Carolinians try to negotiate a treaty from the Cherokee. On August 27, 1774, Henderson and partners signed the Articles of Association of the Louisa Company in Hillsborough in preparation for a possible acquisition.

Henderson decided to lay out a plan using old English court decisions to support his methods of acquiring land from the Cherokee. Westward expansion and making treaties to purchase land with Native tribes by individuals were forbidden by the Crown. Henderson decided to use an old legal decision that related to the East Indians of India, which stated that royal letters were not required "in respect to such places as have or shall be acquired by treaty or grant from any of the Indian Princes or Governments." Some land companies used this decision as a "loop-hole," extending the definition of "Indians" to include American Indians.[43]

Some historians believe that Henderson knew in advance that a "royal grant" would be required to purchase land from the Cherokee. In addition, it was clear that the Proclamation of 1763 forbade settlement west of the mountains, even though the settlements were growing regardless of this fact.[44]

In the winter of 1774–75, Henderson, Boone, and stockholder Colonel Nathaniel Hart traveled from Salisbury, North Carolina, to the Cherokee towns. Henderson made his pitch and proposed his interest in this land purchase, which would be sold to a new company with new partners: Richard Henderson and Company. The company partners solemnly bound themselves as "equal sharers in the property" and vowed to "support each other with our lives and fortunes."

To prove Henderson and Hart's honest intent, Chief Attakullakulla, a young man, and a woman were invited to join Henderson and Hart in North Carolina to inspect all the goods. "When examined, the goods met the complete approval of the natives. The woman examined the goods as acceptable to the women of the tribe."[45]

Of special interest to the Cherokee was the organ, who thought "it must be alive if it could make a sound like that....The organ had to be opened for them, for they heard children inside, who sang....They say they are to receive 4000 pounds in goods....It can hardly be believed."[46]

After inspecting the goods, the Cherokee were satisfied. Before starting back home on January 1, 1775, Henderson arranged a "treaty talk" at Sycamore Shoals in the Watauga settlement. The plan was to begin the festivities on March 1, 1775. Then, on January 6, 1775, Henderson renamed his company the Transylvania Company and added prominent new partners that would deal directly with the Cherokee for twenty million acres. His plan was to set up a fourteenth colony, retain large tracts for personal estates, sell tracts to settlers, charge a perpetual quitrent for every acre sold, and retain special rights in the government.

The journey of Henderson, Cherokee representatives, and others from North Carolina to Sycamore Shoals must have been the talk of the towns that they passed through. Leaving from Cross Creek, North Carolina, they traveled through Flower Gap into Virginia and then followed the Great Road of the Holston to Watauga. "It is said that Henderson rode proudly at the head of the caravan, while Attakullakulla stayed close to the wagons ensuring his people received the goods for the Lands they were selling."[47]

Robert Kincaid, in *The Wilderness Road*, vividly describes the event,

> *Six creaking wagons slowly rumbled down the Great Road past Major Arthur Campbell's broad veranda at Royal Oak in late January 1775. They were heavily laden with merchandise—sacks of corn, flour, salt and casks of rum; bundles of bearskins, duffle, booting, green Durant, Dutch blankets, silver housing, and ribbons; a vast assortment of trinkets of all kinds, shirt metal brooches and wrist bands to catch the feminine eye; a sizeable supply of guns, powder and lead. The goods may well have stocked a half-dozen frontier stores.*[48]

Watauga settlers eagerly awaited the arrival of Henderson, the Cherokee, with the trade goods. *Courtesy of the author.*

Both Cherokee and settlers arrived early, by the hundreds, at the Cherokee's ancient treaty ground at Sycamore Shoals. All were excited to see the vast riches, horse races, and festivities planned for the event. Members of the Watauga settlement prepared much food, including corn, cornmeal, and

This page and opposite: The frontier settlers prepared food and cabins to display goods to be traded for the welcomed arrival of their Cherokee guests. *This page and opposite top*: *Courtesy of the author. Opposite, bottom*: *Courtesy of Sycamore Shoals State Historic Park.*

beef. When Henderson arrived with his six wagons, the goods were displayed in nearby huts built for viewing.

The estimated number of attendees was about 1,200 warriors and 600 Wataugans. According to Williams, "It was not only the greatest event that transpired in their midst, but it was also the most colossal transaction in lands by individuals or a private corporation that America has ever seen. Nearly twenty million acres were involved."[49]

Cherokee chiefs present at the event included Oconostota, the Chief Ruler; Attakullakulla, the Little Carpenter; Willinawaugh, the Great Eagle; Savanooka, the Raven; Onistositah, Corn Tassell; and others. They wore ruffled shirts and leggings, some with gorgets and beads hanging on their chests. Their ears were adorned with bangles. William Bartram, a botanist and naturalist, described Attakullakulla as a "man of superior abilities."[50]

On March 14, the negotiations began. In the interest of fairness, trader Thomas Price offered his services as a language interpreter. He understood the Cherokee language and could interpret accurately, to both sides, what was being said.

Henderson made his proposal: to purchase the Cumberland Valley and the southern half of Kentucky for £10,000 in English money—£2,000 in cash, £8,000 in merchandise. The older chieftains responded favorably, despite some concerns. The goods displayed were tempting, and they had needed more guns and ammo since their 1769 war with the Chickasaw.

The following day, March 15, Henderson further explained his interest in buying the land west of the mountains between the Kentucky and Cumberland Rivers. With great dignity, Attakullakulla stood up to respond. He spoke of how he was an old man and how he presided as chief for over half a century. He reflected on his positive relationship with the king of England and his travels across the "big water." He felt respected by the English and believed he had accomplished his mission successfully. After other comments, Attakullakulla recommended the proposed sale of land, and one by one, other chiefs followed in agreement. One of the older chiefs addressed Boone, saying, "Brother we have given you a fine land, but I believe you will have much trouble in settling it." His comment later became truth in parts of Tennessee and Kentucky.

Tsi'yu gunsini, or Dragging Canoe, the young son of Attakullakulla, the Little Carpenter, was angered as he saw the elders "giving away" their ancestral lands. He made an impassioned speech talking about the strength of the Cherokee before the white man and how other nations had given up land and "melted away like balls of snow in the sun." He raged at the white men

Above: Richard Henderson signs the Great Grant with the Cherokee at the Transylvania Purchase for about twenty million acres of land. *Courtesy of Sycamore Shoals State Historic Park.*

Left: The signature page of the Watauga Purchase, which provided for the Watauga settlers' purchase of their leased land. *Courtesy of Sycamore Shoals State Historic Park.*

and their greed for land and predicted the extinction of his race if they sold their hunting grounds. He asked if buying this land would be enough for the "long knives," sensing "they would surely press for more." Much confusion arose after he spoke. To calm the people, food was brought out while those in attendance spoke among themselves.[51]

The next day, everyone gathered, and the chiefs accepted the proposal. In total disagreement, Dragging Canoe pointed a finger to the Kentucky west and spoke: "A dark cloud hangs over this land, and its settlements will be dark and bloody." With that, he walked purposefully out of the council and "brought the conference to a startling and abrupt conclusion."[52]

On March 17, 1775, the deal, for £10,000 in cash and merchandise, was finalized. The "Great Grant," also referred to as the Transylvania Purchase and the Treaty of Sycamore Shoals, was signed. It included the entire Cumberland River watershed plus the southern half of the Kentucky River watershed, about twenty million acres, and was secured by Henderson's Transylvania Company. The treaty was the largest private, or corporate, real estate transaction in the history of America at the time.

After the success of the first negotiation, the Watauga settlers hoped to purchase the lands that they were currently leasing from the Cherokee. Two days later, on March 19, Henderson and John Williams, who are believed to have drawn up the deed for the Watauga Purchase, offered the Cherokee additional goods if they would sell this land to the Watauga settlement. The Cherokee agreed, and the settlers bought their leased land plus additional acreage for £2,000 of English money and goods. Their purchase included land south of the Holston and Virginia line and the headwaters of the New River, including present-day Watauga, Ashe, and Alleghany Counties in North Carolina, amounting to two thousand square miles.[53]

As the gathering drew to a close, Henderson requested what became known as the Path Deed, which was agreed to between the Holston settlements and Transylvania to safely move settlers through the Cumberland Gap into Kentucky. Carter requested a tract of land from the Cherokee and said he would forgive their debt to him of about £700 for looting his store in Carter's Valley, but the Cherokee refused. Henderson stepped in and said he would destroy the account records of Carter and Parker's store plus trade for, in eighteenth-century terms, "2,000 weight" (close to 2,240 pounds in Britain's standard terms) in leather goods furnished by Robert Lucas, Carter's new partner. Carter then received a deed from Henderson to a portion of the land in Carter's Valley, included in the Path Deed.[54]

A map of the colonies showing the land of the Transylvania Purchase, along with the location of the borders that made up King George's Proclamation of 1763, an imaginary line representing the boundary that colonists were not to cross. *Courtesy of Essyx Design & Fabrication.*

Charles Robertson followed up by buying a large tract in the valley of the Holston, Watauga, and New Rivers on behalf of the Watauga Association for £2,000. Just over a week later, Jacob Brown negotiated the purchase of land on the Nolichucky in two transactions. His land now adjoined the Watauga on both sides of the Nolichucky River from Camp Creek to the Alleghenies on the east, with a cost of £1,700 and forgiveness of debts amounting to £1,500.

On April 1, Charles Robertson, trustee, opened a land office to execute deeds, which were written in the Wataugah Purchase Book, now called Old Book A. James Smith served as land office clerk and William Bailey Smith as surveyor. Sales proceeded first for those who contributed to the purchase cost of the lands until they were paid off. Some lands were reserved for the good of the community via the Petition of 1776. Deeds were granted to the leadership of the Watauga Association, their neighbors, and new families. Most tracts were 200- to 400-acre parcels for individual families, while others were quite large. Folks like Robert Lucas, John Carter, John

Sevier, James Robertson, and Charles Robertson bought multiple parcels. Even Isaac Lincoln, the great-uncle of Abraham Lincoln, bought 303 acres in 1775. Their range ran from the south and north side of the Watauga, along Stoney Creek towards Shady Valley of the Holston Range, the Doe River to the mouth of Watauga, south to the Holston, and up Roan Creek to the northeast.[55]

A week before the signing of the primary treaty, Daniel Boone departed Sycamore Shoals with more than forty axe men, blazing a trail into the wilderness. They worked beyond Long Island of the Holston to the Cumberland Gap and into Kentucky.

In April, Henderson, leading the first settlers, followed Boone's trail to the banks of the Kentucky River, where Boonesborough was founded. Of interest is that Alexander Cameron was following, hoping to catch up with Henderson and arrest him. The next month, outside their stockade, settlers set up a proprietary government and selected delegates to the Second Continental Congress in Philadelphia. By the end of 1775, Kentucky had welcomed three hundred settlers who traveled Boone's Wilderness Trail; others arrived from the north via the Ohio River.

William S. Lester, who wrote *The Transylvania Colony* (1935), addressed the difference between a treaty and a deed in the eighteenth century. National governments or groups granted legal power were the only entities that had the right to make a treaty. Seven of the nine members of the Transylvania Company were deeded land, so each held one-eighth parts; the last two members each held one-sixteenth parts. The final "deed" was signed by three chiefs and eight witnesses.

Colonial leadership, on the other hand, was a little taken back by Henderson's negotiations. North Carolina official Archibald Nelson wrote to a contemporary, "Pray, is Dick Henderson out of his head?" Royal Governor Martin of North Carolina stated Henderson's actions were "illicit and fraudulent" and "of a most alarming and dangerous Tendency," which would help the Natives "in annoying His Majesty's subjects."[56] George Washington stated, "There is something in that affair which I neither understand, nor like, and wish I may not have cause to dislike it worse as the mystery unfolds."[57]

Governor Lord Dunmore issued a proclamation indicating that if Henderson or others tried to settle these lands, they might be required to relinquish their possessions; otherwise, they would face fines and imprisonment. Dunmore then wrote to the Cherokee asking them to "rescind their bargain" as the king did not permit them to give land titles to private persons. To discourage settlers from following Henderson and others, Dunmore charged Colonel William Preston with dispersing copies of his proclamation across the backcountry. Clarence W. Alvord, in *Virginia and the West*, notes that Dunmore had a personal interest in owning and developing lands to the west, which may have played a part in his displeasure with Richard Henderson.

Amid a flurry of reactions, it has been stated that Henderson's hope was to create a fourteenth colony, similar to the other colonies. When addressing the Continental Congress of 1775, the Transylvania Company took care to request that Transylvania be added to the number of the United Colonies. In *Tennessee, the Volunteer State*, John T. Moore indicates, "Henderson was not successful in founding his 'state' in Kentucky. Virginia refused to recognize the validity of his purchase, yet they rewarded him by giving him 200,000 acres of his own selection in Kentucky. North Carolina also granted him and his associates 190,000 acres located in Powell's Valley."

Despite so many leaders denouncing the Treaty of Sycamore Shoals, it appeared that some were also interested in land acquisitions. The legislatures of both Virginia and North Carolina accepted land as part of their own states and extended their boundaries. Much later, after the Revolutionary War, those fighting against the British received land warrants for wartime service from land purchased via the Treaty of Sycamore Shoals.

In addition to being the largest private or corporate real estate transaction in America, the Transylvania purchase stimulated migration by opening central and southwest Kentucky to settlement. As a result, drastic changes in relationships between Native tribes and settlers quickly took place and often escalated into attacks on the settlements. Dragging Canoe and the Chickamauga Cherokee continued to fight for the British, hoping to slow down the westward expansion of white settlers, though they often refused to coordinate with the British troop movements during the American Revolution. The British saw value in their attacks and continued to furnish them arms, ammo, and trade goods.

Attakullakulla, also known as the Little Carpenter, worked toward his lifelong goal of promoting peace between his people and the settlers, which began in 1760 during the Anglo-Cherokee War. He became the tribe's First Beloved Man in 1761 and continued to work toward his goals in this role until approximately 1775. After the 1775 land purchases, followed by the outbreak of the American Revolutionary War, his work for peace seemed to fall apart. In addition, the remainder of this year quickly saw colonial and British relations becoming increasingly worse.

Chapter 6

THE CHEROKEE SIEGE OF FORT WATAUGA, 1776

The Cherokee attacks of July and August 1776 on the settlements of the Watauga, Nolichucky, Holston, and Carters Valley began in an attempt to regain land sold to the settlers during the Treaty of Sycamore Shoals in 1775.

Hoping to prevent attacks on the Watauga settlement, Indian Agents Henry Stuart and Alexander Cameron wrote a letter to the inhabitants of Watauga and Nolichucky on May 7, 1776. Their goal was to oversee a peaceful removal of the settlers to Florida or other lands east of the mountains. The settlements were informed that the Cherokee were inclined to go to war to regain their land sold to the whites by the elders of the tribe. Stuart and Cameron warned the settlers of the danger they would be in if they stayed and that their families would be exposed to a "Mercyless and enraged Enemy." Their letter ended with: "The Indians expect that you will be removed in twenty days."[58]

The people of the Watauga and Nolichucky knew Stuart was in the process of arming the Cherokee and that Virginia had refused to help the Wataugans. So on May 13, Chairman Carter responded, pretending to show loyalty to the British crown and indicating that the settlers intended to move if given extra time to do so. Carter's request for twenty more days was approved, increasing their deadline to forty days, which gave the settlers time to plan.

Despite the warnings, the Watauga and Nolichucky settlers really had no intention of leaving; rather, they intended to use the extra time to

The Watauga settlers were warned of an imminent attack by the Cherokee if they did not leave their land to move back to the British colonies. They did not plan to leave, so plans were made for protection. *Courtesy of Sycamore Shoals State Historic Park.*

prepare for their defense in the event of a Cherokee attack. Hastily, they began constructing Fort Watauga (also called Fort Caswell) and Fort Lee and gathering arms, ammo, and supplies to sustain those taking refuge at the forts.

Thinking the Wataugans might join the British in fear of being destroyed by the Cherokee, Colonel William Christian of Virginia was most likely pleased when the Watauga militia joined him and his militia as they fought against the British. In late June, Virginians from Fincastle County sent a request for a meeting—or a "talk," in Cherokee terms—to the Cherokee in support of the Wataugans. The Virginians stated that the "Cherokee chiefs should find a way to control Dragging Canoe and rid themselves of their British advisors." If they did not agree to a face-to-face talk about this, an invasion of the Cherokee country could be expected.[59] When the Virginians' message was received, it had the opposite of the intended effect and resulted in fueling the fire of war; Dragging Canoe painted himself black and struck the war pole.

To the Honorable the president, and Gentlemen, of the Congress of North Carolina

The Petition of the Inhabitants of Washington District Humbly Sheweth

That on the Nineteenth day of March One thousand Seven Hundred and Seventy Five, on [illegible] We procured A Grant of a small tract of Country Contained within the following bounds To Wit

Begining on the South or South West Side of Holston River, Six English miles above the Long Island in Said River, thence a direct line Near a S. West Course to the ridge which devides the Waters of Wattauga from the Waters of Nolachucky Thence along the Various Courses of Said Ridge, Nearly a South East Course to the blue Ridge, or line dividing No. Carolina From the Cherokee lands, thence along the Various Courses of Said Ridge to the Virginia line, then West along the Virginia line to Holston River, Thence down the Meanders of Holston River, to the first Station, Includeing All the waters Of Wattauga, part of the Waters of Holston, and the head branches of New River or Great Canaway, Agreable to the bounds Aforesaid, of the Cherokee Nation of Indians, that in Consequence of said purchase We have Settled thereon, and before the pres[ent] Indian War, Were Increased to Near the Number of Fifteen Hundred [illegible] of Our [illegible], And [illegible] adjacent Claim Made by One Jacob Brown On Nolachucky River — That being Without the Jurisdiction of Courts then Before Established, the Petitioners Were from Necessity Obliged to Incorporate and form A Society Among Our selves Regulated by Certain Laws or Agreements from time to time, Made for that purpose, That we are True friends to America And that we are Willing to Stand or fall With Our Brethren of the United Colonies — That we appre[hend] and We are Within the Chartered bounds of North Carolina And are desirous to be taken into and Considered as a part of that province Subject to the Ordinances and directions of the Honorable the Convention thereof — And Amenable To the Courts of Justice to be Established by Authority of the Same — That for these purposes And to Obtain a Satisfactory Confirmation of the before Mentioned Grant, And by advice of the Honorable the Council of Safety of Said Province, have Ventured to Chose, Messieurs John Sevier Jacob Womack Charles Robertson John Carter & John Haile, delegates to represent Us in provincial Congress, that as We are Situated On the Western Side of the Mountains And Chiefly Compose the Frontier of the whole province of North Carolina, and are A Weak & defenceless people exposed to the Depradations of Several Nations of Indians, And Many Other Hardships & Inconveniencies, We your Petitioners humbly Implore, that these Our Delegates, may be Received & admitted to Vote in the Honorable the Convention, and that part of the Country now Call Washington district, may be erected into A separate County of North Carolina, And such Other Matters and things with Respect to your Petitioners, As you the Honorable Convention May in your Great Wisdom deem Just and Necessary —

And we Your Petitioners as in duty bound Shall ever pray &c.

Felix Walker
Robert Sevier
Saml. Sherrill Senr.
Vall. Sevier Jr.
Tho. Houghton
Samuel Sherrill
Adam Sherrill
Jacob Brown
J. Smith
Groves Morris
Robert Moseley
Emmanuel Carter
Robert Bean
Martha Mitchell
Joel Mitchell
Joshua Haughton
William Bates
William Tipton
John Easley
John Bumpass
John Odell
William Brocas
Landon Carter
John Brown
Jacob Chandlee
Peter McMial
George Hart
William Clark
Isaac Wilson
William Cloffin
Matthew Hawkins
John Grey
Robert Miller
Samuel Morris
Thomas Cobb
George Russell
Andrew Thompson
John Russell
George Russell Senr.
Samuel Weaver
Richard Bennett
Absalom Thomas
David Crockett
Jonathan Tipton
John Dunham
Jas. Dunham
John McCormack
Lewis Jones
Thomas Dedmon
Humphary Gibson
Elijah Robertson
Hugh Blair
Julius Robertson
Henry Bates
Brooks Robertson
Henry Lyle
David Hughes
James Dunham
Michael Hider
Joseph Greer
Henry Bates Jr.
John Moore
Elexander Cooper
Charles Robertson Senr.
John Robertson
Jordan Reeves
Joseph Brown
William Dodd
Thomas Hughes
George Sherrill
John Davis
Henry Blevens
William Lowbery
Frederick Vaun
Wm. Parker
Thomas Simpson
William Roberts
Charles McCartenee
James McCartinee
Charles McCartinee Senr.
John Carolmy
Charles Hampton
Christer Choate
Aaron Pinson
John Pinson
Thomas Shurley
Joseph Pinson
Aaron Pinson
Zach. Pinson
John Shurley
Thomas Pinson
Edward Shurley
Thomas Jornkins
Benjamin
John Burk
Edmund Russell
John Quinn
William Gyorth

This looming threat enhanced the Wataugans' realization of the need for protection and support from outside of Watauga. The settlement requested that Virginia accept them as part of Virginia, but they were denied. They then reached out to North Carolina, submitting a petition to request annexation on July 5, 1776—the day after the Declaration of Independence in Philadelphia was signed. The petition was signed by the Washington District Committee and one hundred others, with assurances of their commitment and desire to "share in the glorious cause of liberty, enforce our laws under authority and in every respect become the best members of society." John Carter and George Russell delivered the petition to Halifax, where a new council of state was administering the government.[60]

In the meantime, Henry Stuart, with Captain Nathaniel Gist, left Mobile, Alabama, and delivered thirty horse-loads of ammunition to Dragging Canoe and around eighty Cherokee on the Tennessee River. According to Hamer, "The British Agents were convinced that the Cherokee would fight when called upon."[61]

Men from Watauga were sent to Virginia to request help from William Preston in Fincastle, Virginia. With the request was a letter reportedly written by Henry Stuart indicating that the "natives would fight to take back their frontier lands in Virginia and North Carolina." Stuart's letter confirmed that the "Cherokee, in the interests of the British, were being incited to attack the frontier supporters of the American Revolution." Stuart, though, indicated that the letter was a forgery. Whether it was or not, the settlement needed to prepare for a possible attack by the British, who were supported by Cherokee, Creek, and Choctaw allies along with up to five hundred Loyalists living west of the mountains.[62] In response to an anticipated attack, Captain James Robertson's unit joined Captain John Shelby's company and went to approximately seventy Loyalist homes, requiring them to sign an oath of allegiance to the Patriot cause.

Colonel William Russell's Virginia militia had rangers en route to Watauga, but they met up with a party of forty Cherokee fifty miles east of Long Island of the Holston, thus arriving late. Evan Shelby also sent one hundred men on horseback, but the Watauga siege had ended before their arrival. Shelby continued to the Nolichucky to assist and discourage further attacks.[63]

Opposite: The settlers requested protection and support from North Carolina and sent a petition on July 5, 1776, requesting annexation. The Watauga Petition to North Carolina was signed by the Washington District Committee and one hundred others. *Courtesy of Sycamore Shoals State Historic Park.*

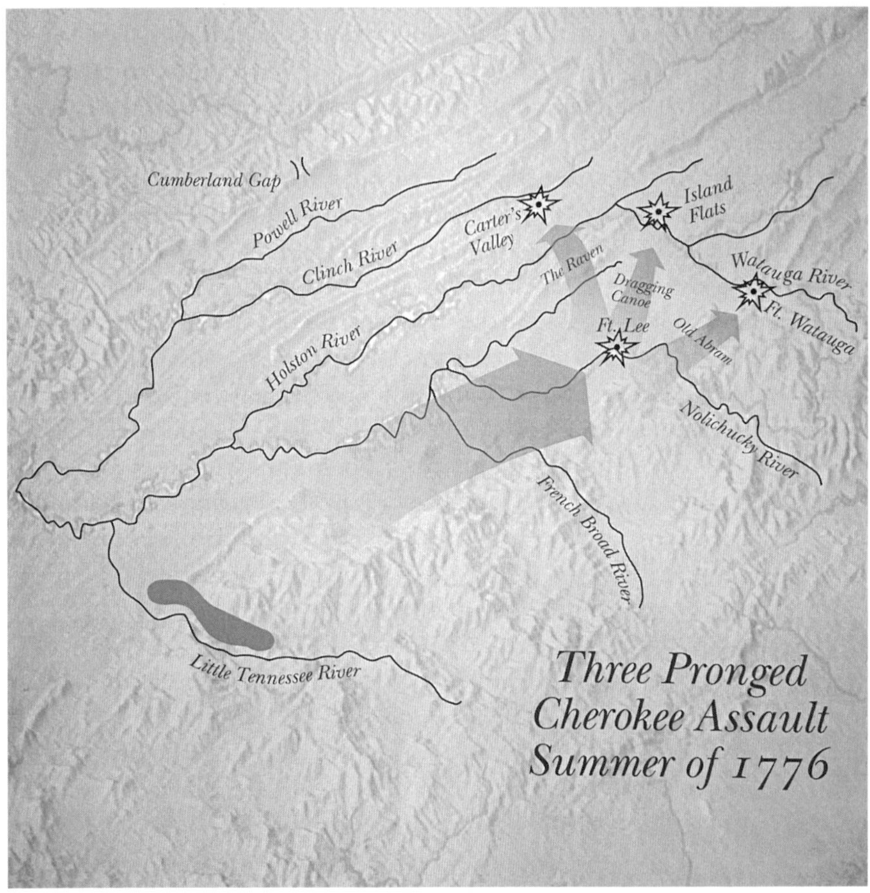

The three attacks on the Watauga, Nolichucky, and Holston were led by three chiefs: Dragging Canoe, the Raven, and Old Abram. *Courtesy of Sycamore Shoals State Historic Park.*

The expected Cherokee attacks on the settlements of Watauga, Nolichucky, and Holston were three-pronged, executed by approximately seven hundred Natives from the Overhill Towns, who were broken down into three commands and aided by the British. These attacks occurred later in July, after the July 1, 1776 attack by Lower and Middle Town warriors on areas in North and South Carolina, during which an estimated two hundred settlers were killed.

Before the attack on the Watauga settlements occurred, General Charles Lee was orchestrating a response to the situation in the Carolinas. His July 7 letter to the North Carolina Council of Safety strongly stated the situation in the Carolinas: "The outrages committed by the Cherokees…must be construed as the commencement of a War." He continued that the plan laid down by "Majesty George the Third is to lay waste the Provinces, burn the habitations and mix Men Women & Children in one common carnage by the hands of the Indians." Lee continued with a retaliatory plan: "To crush the evil before it arises to any dangerous height."[64]

In the Overhill towns, Nancy Ward, after learning of the planned attack at Watauga, most likely assisted four traders, who were being held by the Cherokee, in escaping so they could warn the settlers of Watauga. Ramsey writes that Ward "obtained knowledge of their plan of attack, and without delay communicated it to Isaac Thomas, a trader," who set out for the Holston to warn of the danger. A letter from John Sevier, written from Fort Lee to the officers of Fincastle County on July 11, stated, "Isaac Thomas, Wm. Falling, Jarot Williams and one more, have this moment come in by making their escape from the Indians, and say six hundred Indians and whites were to start for this fort and intend to drive the country up to New River before they return." Nancy Ward was the Beloved Woman of the tribe; her father was a British officer who married the sister of Attakullakulla. Nancy's husband was Bryant Ward.[65]

Chief Dragging Canoe attacked the settlement at Long Island of the Holston. During the altercation, the Holston militia at Eaton's Fort moved out and defended their position, seriously wounding Dragging Canoe.

The chief called the Raven planned to destroy settlements along the Clinch River and Carter's Valley. Many settlers managed to escape, but the Raven burned and pillaged into southwest Virginia.

Chief Old Abram of Chilhowee planned to attack the Nolichucky and Watauga settlements. When he arrived on the Nolichucky, he found that the settlers had left for Watauga. Lieutenant John Sevier had hoped to complete Fort Lee near the Nolichucky River on nearby Limestone Creek, but that was not to be. The warning from the four traders who had escaped from the Natives of imminent attack had reached Sevier. Six hundred natives and whites were heading to Fort Lee. Thus, the Nolichucky settlers headed to Fort Watauga.

On July 21, 1776, a "fierce assault on Fort Watauga began in the early morning." When the attack began, there were some women and children out milking the cows. The fort's defenders were quickly alerted by their screaming as they ran to the fort while being chased by the Cherokee. By the time Catherine "Bonnie Kate" Sherrill got to the fort, the gate was shut. She later commented that she was determined to scale the palisade walls. S.C. Williams writes that she later said, "The bullets and arrows came like hail.

Left: This section of Richard Luce's painting *Cherokee Siege of Fort Watauga*, displayed as a wall mural in the park museum, beautifully and accurately illustrates the appearance of Cherokee warriors in the eighteenth century. *Courtesy of Sycamore Shoals State Historic Park.*

Below: As the attack on Fort Watauga began, Catherine "Bonnie Kate" Sherrill did not get back in time and had to climb the fort wall. John Sevier caught her as she came across to safety. *Courtesy of Sycamore Shoals State Historic Park.*

It was now leap or die for I would not live a captive." Thus, "She threw her bonnet and then herself and clambered over the picketing." Clearing the fort wall, she fell into the arms of John Sevier.[66] Though John was defending the Watauga fort, his family was "forted" at John Shelby's fort in what is now Sullivan County. Four years later, after the death of Sevier's first wife, Catherine became his second.[67]

Leading up to the Fort Watauga siege, Old Abram's warriors captured William Bean's wife, Lydia, who was out riding a horse near the mouth of Boone's Creek on the Watauga River, and took her to the Cherokee base camp on the Nolichucky. While a prisoner, she was questioned by a white man, who was also being held prisoner, at the bequest of the chief. The Cherokee hoped she could give them information about the locations of other settlers' forts, how many people there were, if they had powder, and so forth. After being questioned, she was sentenced to death and taken to a mound to be burned. But the Beloved Woman, Nancy Ward, pronounced a pardon for Lydia Bean and took her to the Cherokee towns so she could teach butter and cheesemaking. Later, Lydia was turned over to Colonel William Christian during his Cherokee Campaign of October 1776.[68]

The attacks continued for two more weeks after Old Abram's first attack, resulting in considerable losses to the Natives. During the repeated attacks, James Robertson's sister Ann Robertson organized a bucket brigade of women who filled buckets with boiling water. The scalding water was poured over the fort wall to stop about twenty-five warriors from setting the fort on fire. Volunteering to pour the water, Ann put herself amid a shower of bullets and was wounded but survived.

Thinking that the Natives had retreated, James Cooper and a boy named Samuel Moore left the safety of the fort with the intention of getting boards to repair a cabin roof in the fort. Before long, Cooper's screams were heard. John Sevier attempted to help him but believed the settlers were outnumbered and that they should not risk the safety of the women and children by leaving the fort to engage with the Natives. The boy, Samuel Moore, was taken captive and was later burned to death. James Cooper's wife, Patience Cobb Cooper, later received a land grant for her husband's service. Because James left the fort during the siege, his actions were considered those of a scouting party and his death attributed to his service during war. As a result, Patience Cooper became the first woman in America to ever hold a land grant in their own name. After her father's death, she also received his three hundred acres on the Watauga River.

Top: The attacks on and defense of Fort Watauga continued for three weeks. *Courtesy of Sycamore Shoals State Historic Park.*

Bottom: Ann Robertson organized a bucket brigade of boiling water to pour over the palisade walls, preventing the fort from being set ablaze. *Courtesy of Sycamore Shoals State Historic Park.*

There are varied reports about how many people were forted at Watauga, in addition to those who defended it. Colonel John Carter, Captain James Robertson, and Lieutenant John Sevier commanded the fort, and William Tatham, an adjutant to their military forces, reported that he was among the seventy-five defenders.[69]

Less than a month after the attacks, reports were published in Williamsburg, Virginia. "Intelligence from Williamsburgh, Virginia," published on August 16, 1776, detailed the depredations endured by the settlers prior to the Siege of Fort Watauga and placed the Indian Wars in regional context, less than one month after the siege:

> *The fort at Watauga, which was besieged by four hundred savages, are now relieved, the Indians having abandoned their enterprise upon the approach of Colonel Russell, with about three hundred men….The fort was thus fortunately relieved (by Colonel Russell) after a fortnight's close siege, during the greater part of which time our people lived on parched corn. There were supposed to be five hundred women and children in this little fort, who fled there for shelter on hearing that the Indians were marching into that part of the country. We lost not a man in this long affair, except four or five who ventured out to drive in some cows; these were found scalped.*

Lyman C. Draper, in his book *Kings Mountain and Its Heroes*, states, "There were a large number of people gathered there [at fort Watauga]."[70] Goodspeed, in *History of Tennessee*, reports that Fort Watauga "contained 150 settlers, including the entire garrison from Gillespie's Station on the Nolachucky below Jonesborough."[71]

Once the attacks ended, all area forts remained garrisoned until Fort Patrick Henry was completed in the Holston settlement. Its construction began in August 1776 and was completed in late September. The fort was planned to garrison over one thousand men.

Just a month after the start of the Cherokee attacks on the Overmountain settlements and almost two months after the July 5 petition requesting annexation into North Carolina arrived at Halifax, North Carolina, the North Carolina Provincial Council addressed it on August 22, 1776.

War with Great Britain was now an immediate threat to the colonies. With that in mind, the Wataugans' petition to North Carolina was positively received, and the Watauga Petition was approved based on their loyalty to the Patriot cause and North Carolina's recognition of the legitimacy of the landholdings in the Watauga settlement. Hence, the Watauga District was

After the Cherokee attacks ended, the Watauga Petition was approved by North Carolina in August. Now, as the threat of war with Great Britain loomed, the Watauga militia began to prepare for what might come next. *Courtesy of the author.*

formed. The same year, the Washington District was designated Washington County, boundaries were adjusted, new counties were created, and a new road was surveyed to cross the mountains, following an old "Indian" road through Yellow Mountain Gap, also called Bright's Trace. In 1777, John Carter was serving as a senator, and John Sevier and Jacob Womack were serving as members of the lower house.

After the Cherokee attacks on the Watauga, Nolichucky, and Holston settlements in 1776, it was evident that the elder chiefs had chosen not to, or maybe were unable to, control Dragging Canoe and his warriors. Thus, retaliation began: Colonial military leaders from Virginia, the Carolinas, and Georgia attacked and burned the Middle and Valley Towns, followed in August by the Overhill Towns.

On May 20, 1777, a peace treaty was signed with the Carolinas and Georgia at DeWitt's Corner in South Carolina, and on July 20, 1777, Little Carpenter and Oconostota signed treaties at Long Island of the Holston with Virginia. Both treaties were written to protect Cherokee towns and end the violence. At the Holston gathering, James Robertson was made Indian agent for North Carolina to the Cherokee. Despite the treaties, members of many Native tribes continued fighting for their lands in two phases. From 1776 to 1783, during the American Revolution, the Cherokee and, sometimes, their allies fought with the British against the settlers.

The first phase of fighting between the American colonists and the Chickamauga Cherokee, who fought for the British, occurred from 1776 to 1783, during the American Revolutionary War. The second phase, after the Revolutionary War, ranged from 1783 to 1794, with Dragging Canoe's Chickamauga Cherokee continuing to fight for their ancestral lands as settlers moved farther to the west. Later treaties, which culminated with the Treaty of Tellico Blockhouse in 1794, ended the Cherokee American wars. During these years of warfare, it is estimated that the Cherokee ceded land in excess of five million acres.[72]

Finding Fort Watauga

Fort Watauga was also referred to in books and letters as Fort Caswell (in honor of North Carolina Governor Richard Caswell), the Watauga Fort, and Carter's Fort since Colonel John Carter was in command.

Information about how long Fort Watauga may have remained standing is documented in books by S.C. Williams and Lyman Draper along with service and pension records after the War of 1812. In *Tennessee During the American Revolution* (1944), Williams writes, "In the late spring of 1777, two companies of North Carolina militia were sent to the western waters to succor the inhabitants on the Watauga and Nolachucky who were being harassed by the Chickamauga's....One company under Captain Benjamin Cleveland was stationed at Fort Caswell, Colonel John Carter being its commander."

Lyman Draper compiled what is now called the Kings Mountain Papers, a collection of letters and documents from the 1740s to the 1810s. From this collection, Draper quoted the service statement of John Yates of Wilkes County, North Carolina. Yates stated that he "volunteered in ranging the country in the Spring of 1777 to keep the Indians in check on the western side of the Blue Ridge under Captain Benjamin Cleveland with their principal station at Carter's Fort." Yates remembered returning home just before harvest.

An 1835 Revolutionary War pension application for Presley Larkins of Floyd County, Indiana, includes a deposition by Robert Macbride on behalf of Larkins. Macbride indicated that he became acquainted with Larkins in 1777 or 1778 when Larkins was enlisted as a fifer. He went on to state that Larkens was blind from smallpox when the two men later saw each other at Tolbert's Fort (Carter's Fort) on the Watauga River.

Near the close of 1777, Colonel G.W. Sevier, the son of General John Sevier, wrote that his father, John, had been appointed lieutenant colonel of the Washington County militia. John Carter served as a colonel in addition to being the entry taker for the county, though he never went out on military campaigns. In addition to Sevier and Carter's roles, the start of 1778 also saw Charles Robertson serving as first major and Jacob Womack as second major.[73]

It can only be assumed that the fort was no longer in existence in 1780 when the Overmountain Men mustered at Sycamore Shoals. All surviving records and correspondence associated with the 1780 muster make no mention of a fort.

As years passed after the siege, information on the location of the fort and what it looked like, along with details of the attacks, were passed down through oral history, letters, and even newspapers of the time.

Describing the fort's location, J.G.M. Ramsey reports, "The Watauga Fort was erected upon the land once owned and occupied by an old settler, Matthew Talbot." Talbot owned the five-hundred-acre fort tract until he sold it to Joseph Tipton Sr. on November 24, 1788.

Ramsey goes on to describe the fort's location as being on a knoll beside the 1853 site of Mrs. Eva Gillespie's house about a half mile northeast of the mouth of Gap Creek. At the writing of Ramsey's book, *Annals of Tennessee*, a few graves and a large locust tree could be used to pinpoint the fort's location. Near the fort were a courthouse and a jail, made from round poles; one of these structures was converted into a stable in 1782. Ramsey also describes a fort owned by Valentine Sevier Sr., upriver on the north side, and Carter Womack's fort somewhere near the head of the Watauga. Williams, in *Tennessee During the Revolutionary War*, states, "The fort on the Watauga was a larger structure," comparing it to Fort Lee on the Nolichucky.

Major James Sevier, in a letter to Lyman Draper, stated,

> *Around the Watauga Fort was a kind of glade and the Indians could approach nearest the fort on the north shore of the river, which was skirted with trees. Behind these the chief portion of the enemy posted themselves,*

Above and left: Archaeological work was completed at the original fort site, providing evidence for its original structure. This information guided the State of Tennessee in planning a re-creation of Fort Watauga for the newly formed state park. *Courtesy of Sycamore Shoals State Historic Park.*

> *one got behind a tree which forked only a few feet from the ground, and watching for an opportunity, the warrior shot when Sevier peeped through a port hole. To Sevier's good fortune, the ball struck in the timber but an inch or so from the hole.*

Searching for evidence of the location of the fort in the summer and fall of 1973, Carl Kuttruff, archaeologist for the State of Tennessee, Division of Archaeology, Tennessee Department of Conservation, conducted a study of the fort site; his final report was released in 1974. He located the site on a "low knoll on the south side of G Street, approximately 100 yards west of the Daughters of the American Revolution, Sycamore Shoals Monument, on the west side of Elizabethton, Tennessee."

Kuttruff's study and archaeological excavations revealed the "east, south, and southwest walls of the fort and a large trash pit just outside the south wall." Despite much testing at the site, other walls or structures were not found. Around 1914, the knoll was landscaped and G Street, the present road, was cut out, which probably destroyed other evidence of the fort's structure.

There were some interesting features found, such as the diameter and spacing of the fort's gateposts: One was 18.72 feet in diameter and a second was 14.82 feet, with 8 feet between them. Kuttruff and his team also found three wall trenches, used to install upright posts to make the fort walls, measuring ninety-nine, fifty-two, and forty-eight feet in length, respectively.

The final report of Kuttruff's study stated,

> [The fort] *probably consisted of an irregular shaped stockade wall connecting several houses, and…there may have been five or six walls surrounding the top of the low knoll on which it was located. The fort walls were made of upright posts which formed the trenches found by the archaeologists but the ends of the three walls located do not meet at the corners, therefore it would be reasonable to assume that some type of house was located in the gaps between the walls.*

Additionally, research completed in May 1974 by Pollyanna Creekmore and Muriel C. Spoden for Sycamore Shoals provided added information on the fort location. They found land records showing that the fort site property was first a five-hundred-acre tract that was owned by Meshech Hale, prior to January 1778, on North Carolina Warrant 349/Land Grant 216. The land, which bordered Talbot's homeplace and Ralph Humphries (now Sycamore Shoals), was transferred to Matthew Talbot on January 28, 1778. Yet J.G.M. Ramsey states, "The Watauga Fort was erected upon the land once owned and occupied by an old settler, Matthew Talbot."

Based on Kuttruff's archaeological findings and the Creekmore/Spoden research, the building of Fort Watauga at Sycamore Shoals State Historic Park was created.

The original site of the fort is located on G Street in Elizabethton and is marked by a monument erected by the Daughters of the American Revolution.

Chapter 7

EVENTS LEADING UP TO THE AMERICAN REVOLUTION IN THE SOUTH

The countries that were the most successful in establishing colonies on lands that now make up the United States were the Spanish, French, British, and Dutch nations. Competing for the control of land resulted in a never-ending flurry of issues, disagreements, treaties, skirmishes, and battles. Altercations arose between the Europeans and Indigenous people who strongly objected to settlers moving westward. As the colonists became disgruntled with the negative actions toward them taken by the British, tensions increased, resulting in ever-growing disagreements. Those loyal to Britain, along with the Cherokee and other tribal members, took up arms against those who opposed the Crown. The Indigenous people anticipated that their support of the British would keep the colonists in the British-controlled colonies, in lieu of moving westward across Native lands.

As early as 1730, the British were building alliances with the Cherokee. The Treaty of 1730 was a significant agreement between the Cherokee Nation and the British. At this time, disputes between the British and the French centered on land control in the Ohio River Valley and other parts of the colonial frontier. In this treaty, the Cherokee pledged allegiance to the British Crown and agreed to fight alongside the British against the French and those allied with the French. In turn, the Cherokee were promised trade benefits and protection of their villages.

Amid the flow of emigration, the French and Indian War, also known as the North American phase of the Seven Years' War, started in 1754; it lasted until 1763. It began over a dispute between the British and the French about

Land claims before and after the French and Indian Wars: 1754 (*before, left*) and 1763 (*after, right*). *Library of Congress, Geography and Map Division.*

RENCH AND INDIAN WARS

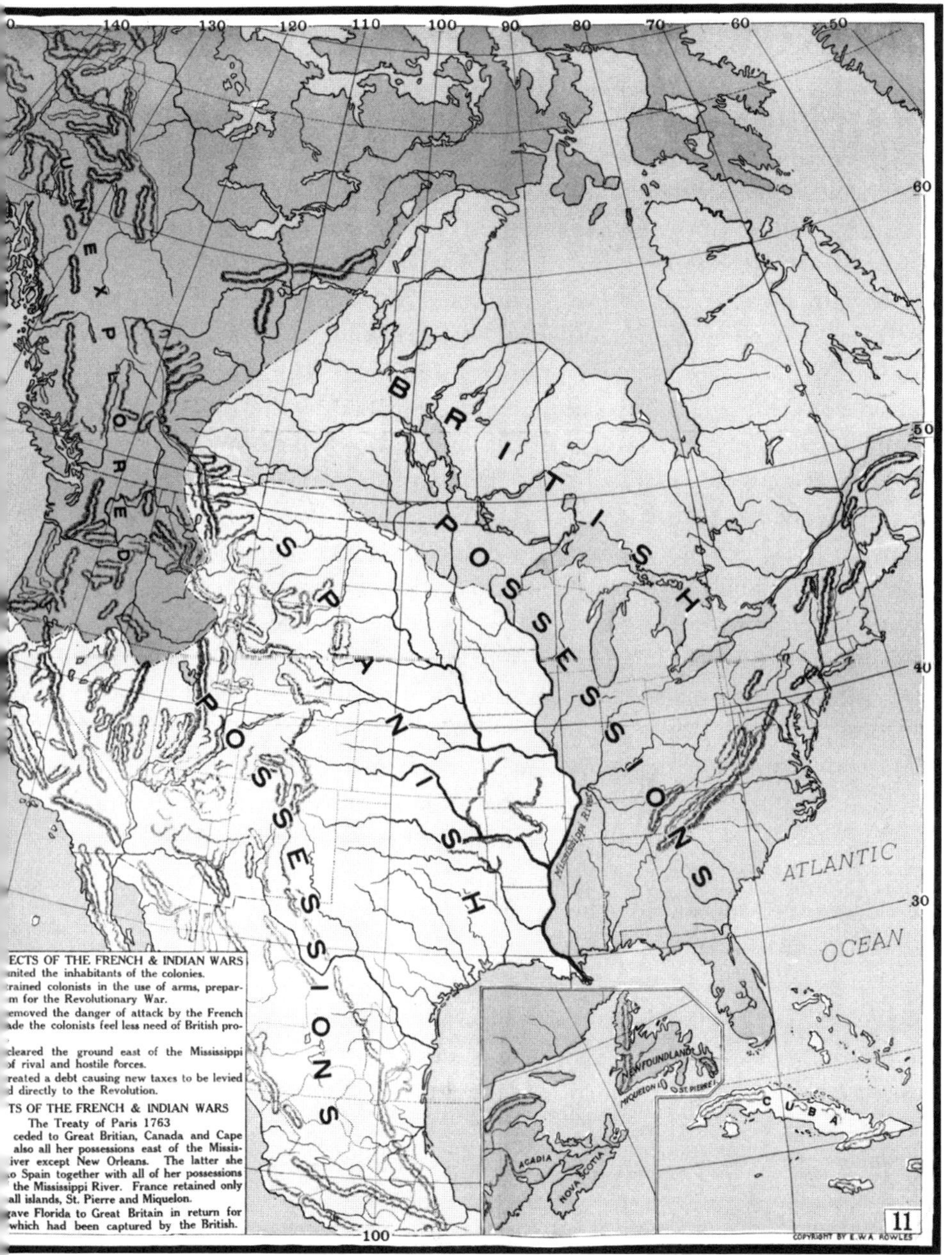

who had control over the trade routes of the Ohio River Valley at the "Forks of the Ohio." George Washington's surprise attack on a small French force at Jumonville Glen, Pennsylvania, in May 1754 ended in high casualties for the French. This skirmish was a catalyst for the start of the French and Indian War. Washington then built a simple fort, Fort Necessity, which was attacked in July 1754 by a large French and Indian force. There, Washington surrendered for the first—and only—time in his career.

Both the British and the French were trying to gain support from Native tribes in the area. Some allied with the British and some with the French. The British invoked the earlier Treaty of 1730, which provided for the Cherokee's allegiance to the British and their agreement to fight alongside the British. The Cherokee were promised trade benefits and protection of their villages through construction of forts defended by the British. South Carolina built Fort Prince George in 1754 in Keowee in the Lower Towns of the Cherokee but did not provide for defense of the fort or other Cherokee towns. In July 1757, Fort Loudoun was constructed near Echota; defense of the fort was a continuing issue. In compliance with the 1730 treaty, the Cherokee continued protecting colonial settlements in the Carolina and nearby colonies for three more years.

With a host of positives and negatives in place, the upper Ohio valley tribes believed supporting the French to be the lesser of two evils. The Cherokee first supported the British against the French but later, feeling they had been treated poorly by the British, began attacking North Carolina frontier colonists, beginning the Anglo-Cherokee War, or the War with Those in the Red Coats (1758–1761). Colonel Archibald Montgomery destroyed five of the Lower Towns but was defeated as he approached the Middle Towns. The Cherokee, considering this a moral victory, attacked and captured Fort Loudoun on August 8, 1760. Then, in June 1761, British regulars, American militia, and Catawba and Chickasaw Indians, under Lieutenant Colonel James Grant, defeated the Cherokee in the Middle Towns, ending the resistance. The Treaty of Charleston, signed in December 1761, ended hostilities between the British colonists and the Cherokee and removed the French from Cherokee lands.

Two treaties followed involving Great Britain in 1763. The Treaty of Paris, signed in February 1763 by Britain, France, and Spain, formally ended the Seven Years' or French and Indian War in North America. It involved complex land exchanges between these nations, including establishing the Mississippi River as the boundary between French and English land to the east—excepting Louisiana, which was ceded to Spain from France. The

British received some French lands overseas, Florida, and Upper Canada. For context, at this time, King George III was the most powerful monarch in Europe; he also had the largest navy.

King George III issued the Proclamation of October 7, 1763, after meeting the three Cherokee chiefs in London. It reserved all lands west of the Appalachian Mountains as Indigenous territory and forbid the king's subjects from making purchases or settlements on these lands. The fear was that as emigrants moved farther west, they would emancipate themselves from English control. As a result, the superintendent of Indian affairs ordered settlers west of the mountains to leave and return to the British colonies.

The French and Indian War also increased disagreements and tensions between the American colonies and the British leadership—not to mention that the British victory resulted in their taking more control over the colonies. Britain had a good deal of war debt, so hoping to recover funds, the British began to tax the colonists and put restrictions on frontier expansion west of the mountains.

In 1764, a hidden Sugar Act tax was included in the cost of import duties for goods sent to the colonies. It was the first tax imposed by the British on the colonies, but the colonists were not aware of it. This tax was implemented to end sugar and molasses smuggling from the French and Dutch West Indies and to recover debt from the French and Indian War.

The Stamp Act of March 22, 1765, was the event that catalyzed the start of the American Revolution. This tax was not a hidden tax and was implemented without allowing the colonists the opportunity to have input. This was the first time that the issue of taxation without representation came to the forefront, which quickly became the common cause that united all thirteen colonies. The Stamp Act provided for a tax on paper items and printed materials, such as newspapers, pamphlets, and licenses, which were required to be stamped with a tax.

The Sons of Liberty, formed by Samuel Adams, organized protests against British policies; riots in Boston ensued. Andrew Oliver, the stamp distributor in Massachusetts, quickly became the target of mob protests. An effigy of Oliver was carried through the streets, hung from the Liberty Tree, and subsequently beheaded. The Liberty Tree was an elm tree that symbolized colonial protest and was a gathering place for those who opposed British policies. Public announcements and banners were frequently posted on or near the tree. Oliver's warehouse property was destroyed, and he soon resigned his role as Stamp Act distributor.

By November 1765, no stamped paper was available, and all activities requiring paper ceased to take place. North Carolina Governor Tryon reported, "All Civil Government is now at a stand." In March 1766, the British Parliament repealed the Stamp Act.

This was not the end of taxation, though. Parliament passed the Townshend Act in 1767, which imposed taxes on imports of glass, paper, lead, pigments, and tea. Again, colonists were encouraged to boycott these goods.

In the south, in 1768, the Regulator movement began in Orange County, North Carolina, protesting taxation and abuses conducted by public officials. This movement grew for just over two years until the Regulators were defeated by Governor Tryon's North Carolina militia at the Battle of Alamance on May 16, 1771.

Samuel Adams was a popularly read publicist who wrote for the *Gazette* newspaper on topics related to liberty. In 1772, he wrote an essay, "The Rights of Colonists," to bring attention to the basic freedoms that the British government were attempting to take from the people. He also created the first Committee of Correspondence, which encouraged its members to communicate their ideas in pamphlets and letters.[74]

During this same period, in 1772, miles away from Boston, occupants of the Watauga settlement were organizing what became the first free and independent government on the continent, the Watauga Association.

Historian Thomas Fleming aptly frames Samuel Adams's talents in his biography: "Without Boston's Samuel Adams, there might never have been an American Revolution. His skill at combining agitation and propaganda put the British constantly on the defensive."[75]

Samuel Adams became the primary organizer of the Boston Tea Party, a protest conducted in opposition to the Tea Act, which was passed in May 1773. The purpose of the Tea Act was to help the British East India Company, which had an overabundance of tea. The Tea Act allowed the company to sell its tea at a lower price to the colonies. Even though the East India Company's tea was cheaper, the British Parliament still taxed the tea in hopes that colonists would accept taxes as the norm. Thus the colonists were expected to pay a tax of three pence per pound of tea. In addition, the British were competing with smuggled and cheaper Dutch tea.

The Tea Act continued the British practice of taxation without representation. When the tea arrived in Boston Harbor on December 16, 1773, colonists dressed as Natives dumped 342 chests of the British tea on the ships into the harbor in opposition to the tax. This rebellion took

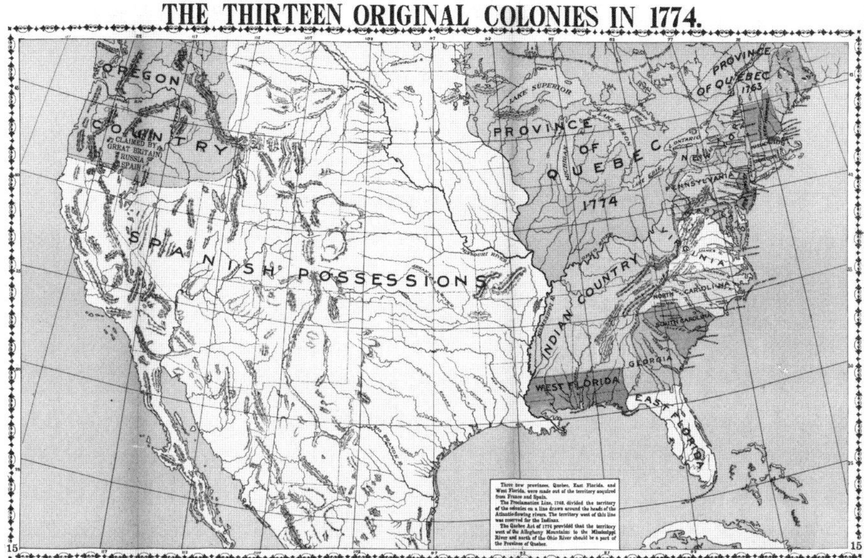

Map of the colonies in 1774. *Library of Congress, Geography and Map Division.*

place just under two years before the Transylvania Purchase occurred at Sycamore Shoals.

The British response came in March 1774 when they closed Boston Harbor via the Boston Port Act until the colonists paid for the tea they destroyed. The Boston Port Act was one of the four "Intolerable Acts," in addition to the Massachusetts Government Act, which revoked the colonial charter and put an appointed government in place; the Administration of Justice Act, which allowed British officials accused of crimes to be tried in Britain instead of the colonies; and the Quartering Acts, which gave British soldiers the right to be housed in private colonial homes.

The effects of these acts were completely the opposite of what the king expected. Instead of obeying the king's Intolerable Acts, the colonies became more united against the king as a common enemy. Rebellion and protest continued, and in early 1774, John Malcomb, a British customs agent, was tarred and feathered by the Sons of Liberty. The Intolerable Acts were perceived as a threat to the colonists' liberties in America, which continued to bring people together in a "common cause for all." The Continental Congress in the fall of 1774 denounced the Intolerable Acts.

From May to October 1774, Lord Dunmore's War was fought, under the command of John Murray, the fourth earl of Dunmore and Virginia's last royal governor. Tensions rose between the Shawnee, their allies, and Virginia leadership as white settlers continued moving to land ceded to Virginia south of the Ohio River. Tribal nations—not recognized by the Shawnee and their allies—had entered into treaties with the white settlers for this land, although the Shawnee had hunted these lands for generations and opposed the settlers' land claims.

The Battle of Point Pleasant on October 10, 1774, brought Lord Dunmore's War to an end. Lord Dunmore formed two armies to attack the Shawnee villages: a northern army led by Dunmore and a southern army led by Colonel Andrew Lewis. Shawnee Chief Cornstalk anticipated this military move and attacked Lewis's troops at Point Pleasant before they merged with the northern army. Supporting Lewis were the Wataugans, led by Captain Evan Shelby, with a company from the Watauga and a second from the Holston. Serving as sergeants were James Robertson and Valentine Sevier Jr.

The engagement between Lewis, the Shawnee, and the Mingo branch of the Iroquois Nation saw brutal hand-to-hand combat. About one thousand troops fought on each side. In the end, Chief Cornstalk had no choice but to cede to Virginia all Shawnee claims to land south of the Ohio River at the Treaty of Camp Charlotte, which opened Kentucky to settlement. Many historians consider this battle the first of the Revolutionary War, as the British actions incited Native discontent with the colonists.

This show of support to the Virginians by the Wataugans at Point Pleasant was the first time the Watauga militia had volunteered to assist its northern neighbors, who had not offered aid to the settlement of Watauga previously. S.C. Williams writes, "The contingent of Wataugans had the added satisfaction of having volunteered their service to a province to which they owed no allegiance."[76]

Just one month after Henderson's Treaty of Sycamore Shoals was signed in March 1775, Paul Revere and others took to horseback on April 18, warning the minutemen in the Province of Massachusetts Bay of the approaching British army. The next day, British troops were sent to Concord, Massachusetts, to seize colonial weapons. Presenting a surprise attack, the Lexington militia tried to stop them, but the British battled their way through and continued to Concord, where they again were surprised by an attack from the Concord militia. There, the British were defeated after losing more than 270 men, while the Concord militia lost less than 100 volunteers. The Battles of Lexington and Concord, whose opening shot was referred to as the Shot Heard 'Round the World, marked the beginning of the American revolutionary war for independence.

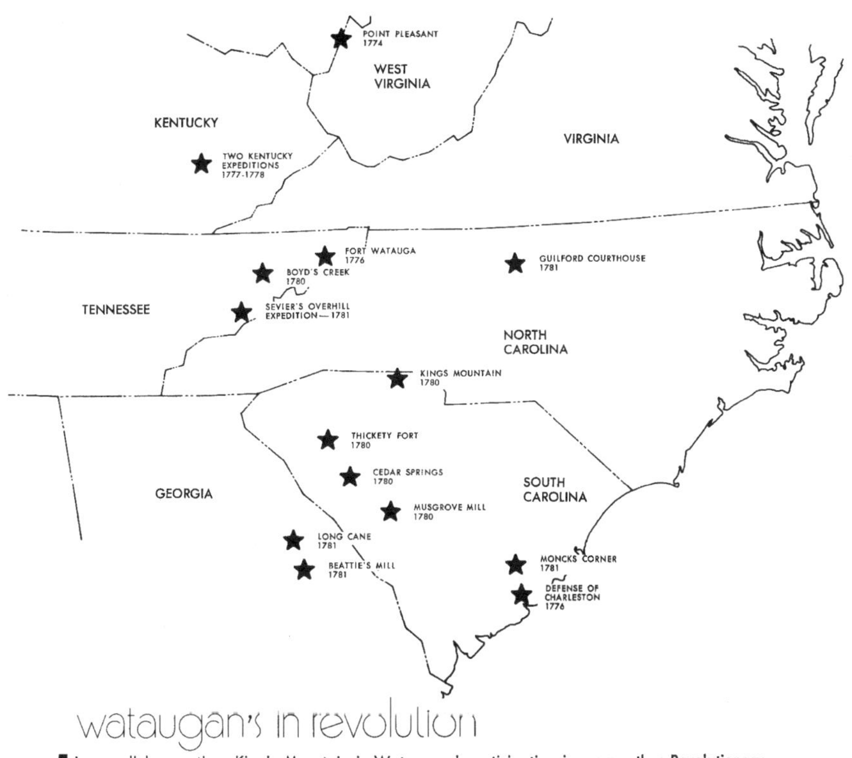

Illustrated on this map are Revolutionary War engagements in which the Watauga, Nolichucky, and Holston militia participated. *Courtesy of Sycamore Shoals State Historic Park.*

In anticipation that the colonies might again need to protect themselves, on June 15, 1775, George Washington was appointed as the commander of the united Patriot forces, known as the Continental Army, which was established on June 14, 1775, by the Second Continental Congress. Just two days after Washington's appointment, on June 17, the Battle of Bunker Hill was fought as British forces attempted to take control of the hills surrounding Boston. Even with over 1,000 casualties for the British and 411 for the Americans, the victory was a British one. The Americans' spirits were boosted nonetheless, and their persistence not to give up was evident.

Delegates of the Congress still hoped to avoid war, so in July, they sent the Olive Branch Petition, promising loyalty to King George III and asking him to remove troops from Boston as a sign of peace. The king did not accept their petition and instead declared on August 23, 1775, that there was a state of rebellion in America, with an underlying message that the British were not going to tolerate the colonists' actions.

Back home on the Watauga, the settlers were evaluating what the outcome of these events might mean to them. They wondered how the Native tribes would react to war, who they would support, and whether they would see this as an opportunity to recover their ancestral lands. There was also the question of how colonists would be divided in their Loyalist support for Britain versus the Patriot cause. There was much at stake for the Wataugans, who were firmly settled in their communities after purchasing their leased land from the Cherokee.

By the middle of 1775, the North of the Holston settlement joined Fincastle County, Virginia, in forming a revolutionary Committee of Safety at Chiswell's Mine. They had a seat in the Second Continental Congress, with Evan Shelby adhering to the national boycott of British goods. In addition, Mecklenburg County citizens in North Carolina drew up a set of resolutions intended to nullify the authority of Great Britain in their colony. This action resulted in colonial Governor Martin fleeing New Bern and a provincial congress meeting in August to set up a revolutionary government.

The Washington County Regiment of the North Carolina Militia and Fife and Drum Corps. *Courtesy of the author.*

These actions prompted the settlers of the Watauga and Nolichucky to meet and agree to support the Patriot cause; they then combined to form the new Washington District and established a Committee of Safety. John Carter, appointed colonel of the district militia, also served as chair of the committee. A later list of committee members included Charles Robertson, John Sevier, James Robertson, William Bean, George Russell, John Jones, Robert Lucas, Jacob Womack, Jacob Brown, James Smith and Zach Isbell. This committee represented the Watauga, Nolichucky, and south of the Holston settlements along with William Bean's community.[77]

The year 1775 also greatly affected the Native people living east of the Mississippi. As fighting continued to grow between the Continental and British armies, both armies hoped for the support of Native tribes. Many supported the British due to their concerns about westward expansion if the British lost, others remained neutral, and some supported the Patriot cause.

Attacks by the Cherokee and other tribes against white settlers became more frequent in 1776. Given the growing number of attacks, the need for the settlers to be prepared to protect themselves became a way of life. The Cherokee were allies of the British, who continued to provide guns, ammunition, and various supplies to them.

On February 27, 1776, at the battle of Moore's Creek, North Carolina, Patriot forces successfully stopped the British advance to the coast near Wilmington. Approaching early summer, the Watauga settlers had been warned of a possible Cherokee attack on their homes and simultaneously learned about a possible British attack on Charleston, South Carolina. Many men remained at the Watauga settlements to protect the home front in the event the Cherokee did attack. Additionally, a small platoon of riflemen was sent to Charleston from the southwest settlements, recruited by Lieutenant Felix Walker. "A company of fine riflemen were accordingly enlisted and put under Captain James Robertson," who marched to the coast, joining a South Carolina regiment. On June 28, 1776, Admiral Peter Parker of the British navy and General Henry Clinton of the British army attacked Sullivan's Island in hopes of capturing Charleston. The ten-hour battle ended in the withdrawal of the British.[78]

In early July 1776, discussions were taking place between military leaders in the south after the July 1 attacks in North and South Carolina by the Lower and Middle Town Cherokee. The possibility that the British might influence the Cherokee and arm them to assist in conquering the southern colonies was a real concern. Before action could be taken, the settlements of

News of the Declaration of Independence probably took several weeks to arrive on the Watauga frontier. *Courtesy of Tim Massey.*

Nolichucky, Watauga, and Holston became aware, no later than July 11, that Cherokee attacks were imminent.

Prior to the July 21, 1776 attacks on the Watauga settlements, General Charles Lee, in command of American forces in Charleston, wrote on July 7 that "the Cherokees should be treated as at war, in aid of the British" in response to the July 1 attacks in North and South Carolina.[79]

Similar messages and plans were supported by leadership in the province of South Carolina, while John Page, president of the Convention of Virginia and the Continental Congress, received similar communications. The final recommendation on July 30 was that "Virginia, North Carolina, and Georgia, cooperating with South Carolina should work together in carrying on a war with all possible vigor against those savages."[80]

President Page applied to North Carolina to send 300 men to join Colonel William Christian's Virginia force in early August as the Cherokee Campaign of 1776 moved into action. Christian's troops, with Colonel Charles Lewis as second-in-command, successfully attacked the Overhill Towns. Colonel Andrew Williamson's South Carolina troops attacked the Lower Towns before a Cherokee attack on South Carolina and Georgia came to fruition. Williamson then joined General Griffith Rutherford in the destruction of the Middle and Valley Towns. The Watauga and Nolichucky troops were commanded by Captains James Robertson and John Sevier and joined up with Colonel Christian, coming together to form a battalion under Major Evan Shelby of a reported 1,800 men. By the fall of 1776, over 50 Cherokee towns had been destroyed.[81]

The Cherokee people signed treaties for peace and had to give up much land that was once part of their oldest towns. Colonel William Christian, the leader of the expeditionary forces, presided over the 1776 treaties in a humane manner, for which he was criticized by some military leaders. Christian chose not to starve the women and children by taking their corn or resort to barbarity. His death came years later when, in 1786, when he was killed leading an expedition against Native tribes on the Ohio. Those known as the Chickamauga Cherokee moved into today's Tennessee and northern Alabama and, until 1794, continued their fight to regain their land.

After Colonel Christian's treaties, during the winter of 1776–77, Dragging Canoe's Chickamaugas became stronger and continued to threaten war with the settlers as their raids continued. Colonel Nathaniel Gist was commissioned to the Continental army in January 1777 and was sent to Fort Patrick Henry to encourage the Cherokee to discuss treaties there. Several chiefs attended and met at Long Island of the Holston on March 20 with commissioners from Virginia. Without the presence of Dragging Canoe, completing a treaty was deemed inadvisable. As Gist attempted to reach Dragging Canoe for a June 26 negotiation, the Chickamaugas continued harassing the Watauga and Nolichucky settlers. Captain Benjamin Cleveland kept troops stationed at Carter's Fort, and Major Jess Walton did the same on the Nolichucky at Fort Williams.

The gathering did come to pass on June 28. Corntassel, who was very well spoken, addressed the group on behalf of his people. Soon after, agreements were made, and new boundaries were determined. Much Cherokee land was ceded to the whites during the July 1777 Treaty of Long Island of the Holston. James Robertson became the Indian commissioner to the Overhill Cherokee for North Carolina, and Joseph Martin filled the same role on behalf of Virginia. William Campbell of Washington County marked the new boundary between the Cherokee and the Virginians during the winter of 1777–78.[82]

Dragging Canoe, on the other hand, refused to participate in the treaties, favoring war against the whites instead. Nearly one thousand Chickamauga

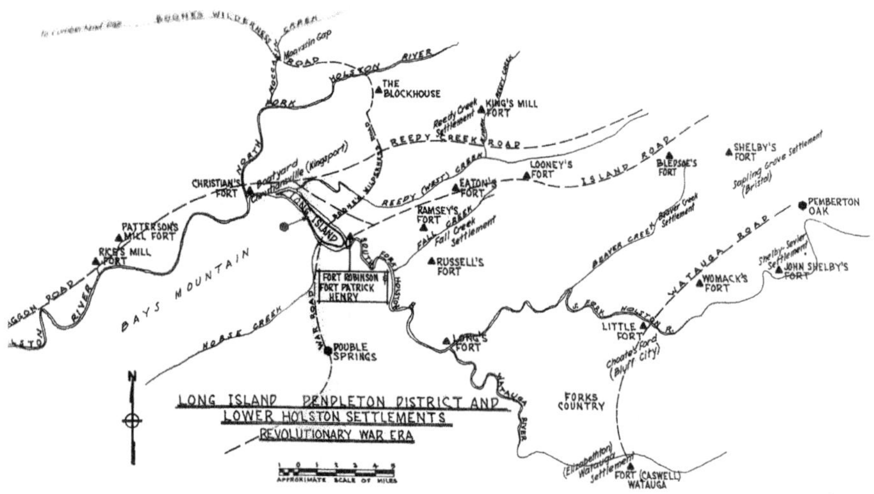

The Long Island and Holston settlements during the Revolutionary War. *Courtesy of Murial Spoden.*

representing tribes from the Ohio gathered at Nickajack Cave, Dragging Canoe's stronghold near the Tennessee-Georgia border on the Tennessee River. Their presence resulted in continued attacks on the settlers in the southwestern settlements. Native tribes remained involved during the American Revolution, attacking Patriots and settlers from Georgia to Pennsylvania along with new settlements appearing even farther to the west.

Patriot leaders Colonels Evan Shelby and John Montgomery set forth on a campaign to Chickamauga in April 1779, leading a force of one thousand men. Other leaders also strove to defeat Dragging Canoe's warriors, but they continued to attack white settlements up until 1794, when their towns of Running Water and Nickajack were destroyed. Dragging Canoe, remembered for his dedication to preserving Cherokee culture and ancestral lands, died in February 1792, after a night of celebration from a victory against the Cumberland settlement, from a possible heart attack.[83]

After Dragging Canoe's death, warfare continued as settlers encroached on Cherokee land. In 1794, the Chickamauga Cherokee notified Governor Blount of their desire to make peace. Their sentiments were echoed by Bloody Fellow at the treaty negotiations who stated, "I want peace, that we may…sleep in our houses, and rise in peace on both sides." During a 1794 gathering at the Tellico Blockhouse, a United States fort built to protect the Cherokee from encroaching settlers, a lasting peace treaty was signed by John Watts, Dragging Canoe's successor.

Chapter 8

THE MUSTER OF THE OVERMOUNTAIN MEN, 1780

As the American Revolution continued, many Native tribes were still waging war on the frontier settlements, and the British were experiencing more losses in the north and involved in military engagements in the south. Evaluating their wins and losses since the start of the war, the British were concerned with rebellion in the north, including their losses at the Battles of Saratoga in New York in 1777; learning that the French were becoming involved in the war; and struggling with their strategy in controlling the Patriots and their militias. Some thought the North would eventually support the British due to positive trade relationships and common industrial advances.

Feeling that New England was probably a lost cause, the British began to shift their efforts to the colonies in the south, anticipating that the southern Loyalists would support the king's war in both the north and the south. What they ultimately found was that the south was more divided than expected.

The British had earlier attempted to seize Charleston, South Carolina, in 1775, which was unsuccessful. The same year, on June 14, 1775, the Continental army was formed, representing the thirteen united colonies. The Southern Campaign of the Revolution officially began when Savannah, Georgia, fell under British control in December 1778.

In February 1780, the Overmountain Men were called on by the North Carolina Council of State to assist in defending Charleston, South Carolina, from the British, who were attempting to capture the city for the second

Lloyd Branson's painting of the muster of the Overmountain Men, completed in 1915. *Courtesy of Tennessee State Museum.*

time. The attempt ended in a British victory, led by General Henry Clinton, and resulted in near-total British control of South Carolina.

In the North and South Carolina backcountry, Patriots were already engaging in guerrilla warfare with Loyalists in "neighbor against neighbor" fighting in strongly divided communities. Local militias formed under

leaders that included Francis Marion, the Swamp Fox; Thomas Sumter, the Gamecock; and Andrew Pickens, the Wizard Owl, in what was referred to as a "bloody civil war."

On May 29, 1780, British Colonel Banastre Tarleton, searching for remaining Continental troops after Charleston, massacred Abraham Buford's men at the Waxhaws while they were attempting to surrender. The following month, General Lord Charles Cornwallis was given command of the Southern Theater when General Clinton left for New York.

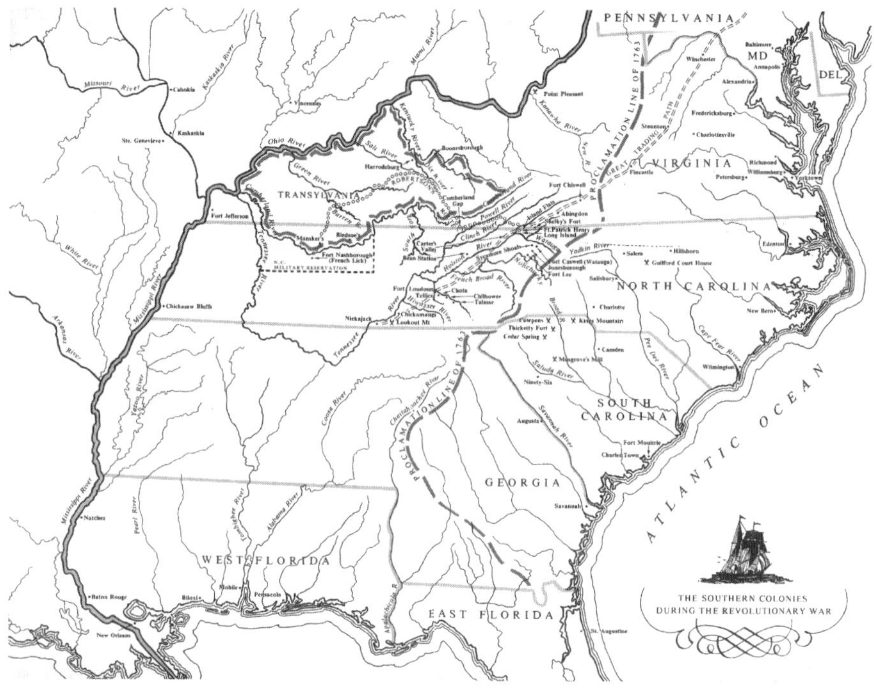

Samuel Cole Williams's map of the Southern Colonies in the Revolutionary War. *From* Tennessee During the Revolutionary War, *1944.*

Patriots commanded by Colonel Isaac Shelby, Colonel James Robertson, and Colonel Elijah Clarke of Georgia, with about six hundred men, quickly overtook Loyalist Colonel Patrick Moore's Thickety Fort in South Carolina with ninety-six men inside. The morning of July 26, 1780, the Loyalists awoke to find they were surrounded. Shelby sent Captain William Cocke to demand they surrender, but Moore replied that he intended to defend his post "to the last extremity." Shelby moved his troops closer, surrounding the fort. Before attacking, Shelby sent a second demand to surrender. Moore agreed to the surrender on the morning of July 30, 1780, if his troops were paroled and did not serve again during the war.[84]

Later that year, after Ferguson's defeat at Kings Mountain in October, a fragment of a draft report related to Thickety Fort written by Colonel Patrick Ferguson to General Cornwallis was found. It stated, in part,

> *The officers next in command, and all others, gave their opinion for defending* [the fort] *and agree in their account that Patrick Moore, after proposing surrender, acquiesced in their opinion....* [Moore] *returned with*

> *some Rebel officers whom he put in possession of the gate and place, who were instantly followed by their men, and the fort was full of Rebels to the surprise of the garrison. He pleaded cowardice, I understand.*

J.G.M. Ramsey, author of *Annals of Tennessee*, possessed the original document. Moore's surrender foiled Ferguson's plan to attack the Patriot troops while they were engaged in taking Thickety Fort.[85]

Major Patrick Ferguson had his first run-in with what the British called the backwater men (Overmountain Men) of the western settlements in early August. Returning to McDowell's camp, the Overmountain Men were quickly sent back out with little rest to track the enemy's movements under Ferguson. The Patriots learned that Ferguson knew of their presence, so they fell back to a site they could defend at Cedar Spring. Ferguson's numbers were high, but his force was not accustomed to fighting in the forest in what was described as a "running fight." The Patriots were quite confident fighting in the same manner as the Cherokee and emerged with fewer captured, wounded, and killed than Ferguson's army, who abandoned their assault after about four or five miles.[86]

Other engagements continued, including an altercation at Camden, South Carolina, on August 16, 1780, when General Horatio Gates was sent to command a newly formed southern Continental army. As Cornwallis arrived at Camden to secure this site for the British, a battle ensued. Gates was defeated, and his army removed to North Carolina to await a new commander. Two days later, Banastre Tarleton defeated Thomas Sumter at the Battle of Catawba Ford.

McDowell became aware of a Loyalist outpost at Musgrove Mill and sent a detachment under Colonel James Williams to join Colonels Isaac Shelby of Watauga and Elijah Clark of Georgia, along with other officers, and Watauga and Nolichucky riflemen who traveled by night to Musgrove Mill. When they arrived, a few scouts came across a small patrol of Tories, and a small skirmish took place. When the British officers became aware of this event, British Colonel Innes succeeded in negotiating the agreement of the other leaders to march out to "bag" this bunch of "ragamuffins" before they retreated.

In the meantime, a local gentlemen informed the Patriots of the British troops' numbers. The outnumbered Patriots decided that neither retreating nor attacking were good choices, so they reorganized on and around a ridge in preparation for an anticipated fight. Their entire force was camouflaged with brush, logs, and trees, which formed one extended line in a semicircle.

Their position gave a good view of the road to Musgrove Mill, where they hoped to lure the Loyalists into an ambush.

Captain Shadrach Inman, with around twenty-five men on horses, was sent to fire on and provoke the British so they would cross the ford, drawing them into the "net which Shelby and Clarke had so adroitly prepared for them."[87]

The riflemen hidden in the brush were ordered not to fire a shot until orders were given. When the British were within seventy yards of the American lines, the Patriots opened fire. Fighting continued as the Patriot troops continued to hold the line, but Shelby's right flank was giving way. Just then, British Colonel Innes was injured, fell from his horse, and was removed from the field, reportedly shot by Wataugan William Smith. Shelby's men then let out a yell and rushed the enemy. The British and the Tories, retreating, were followed by the Overmountain Men. In the heat of pursuit, Patriot Captain Inman was killed during hand-to-hand fighting, shot seven times.

Despite some losses, the sharpshooting skills of the Overmountain Men served them well. In addition to British Colonel Alexander Innes being shot, a captain was killed, and five of the seven surviving officers were wounded.[88]

The commanders of the American troops planned to continue to Ninety-Six, but before they embarked, Major McDowell arrived in great haste with a short letter from Governor Caswell, dated at the battleground, apprising McDowell of the defeat of the American's grand army under General Gates on September 16 near Camden, and advising McDowell "to get out of the way, as the enemy would endeavor to improve their victory… by destroying all small corps of the American army." Shelby, recognizing Caswell's handwriting, knew the letter was not a Tory trick; therefore, he gave warning so that the westerners would travel in the direction of the mountains, moving through the woods to escape. They knew Ferguson and his men would be on their trail, hoping to retake prisoners.

Their quick escape was later recorded by Colonel Shelby—whose letters are now stored as the King's Mountain Letters of Colonel Isaac Shelby in the Southern Historical Collection of the University of North Carolina—as follows,

> *It required all the vigilance and exertion which human nature was capable of to avoid being cut to pieces by Ferguson's light parties….The enemy pursued as was expected fifty or sixty miles, until their horses broke down and they could follow no further….The Americans never stopped to eat*

> *but made use of peaches and green corn for their support. The excessive fateague to which they were subjected for two nights and days so effectively broke down every officer that their faces and eyes swelled and became so bloated in appearance, as scarcely to be able to see.*[89]

En route to the mountains, the Overmountain Men stopped briefly to feed their horses, not certain of Ferguson's whereabouts. Some thirty minutes after their departure, Ferguson's party, which had rapidly been pursuing them, came upon this location, but unaware of how far ahead the Americans were, they ended their pursuit.[90]

Likely confident in the power of his wins, General Cornwallis planned for his takeover of North Carolina, including the western settlements. He moved his troops northward while Tarleton and Ferguson protected his western flank. They also were gathering more Tory forces to cripple the opposition. By July, Ferguson, along with his English regulars and Tories, had gained 4,000 loyalist militia raised near Ninety-Six and an additional 1,500 men raised by Tories near Catawba.

To inform the overmountain people of Ferguson's movements, messengers carried information to and from the Watauga and Holston commanders. It was expected that Ferguson would run out of supplies and stop elsewhere, but he ultimately proceeded on to Gilbert Town, three miles west of present-day Rutherfordton, North Carolina. McDowell was moving north to Burke County, followed by some of Ferguson's men. After a brief skirmish and fearing capture by a stronger force, McDowell and his men, some with their families, traveled across the Blue Ridge to Watauga. McDowell marched 160 men through the Catawba valley and over the mountains until they reached the Watauga settlements. When they arrived, they set up camps and were taken in by their western friends.[91]

The situation was indeed looking grim for the Patriot cause. The leadership of North Carolina stated on October 4 that Cornwallis had taken possession of Charlotte and concluded with a note that Ferguson was also in the state in Burke County.

Feeling the wind behind his sails generated by British successes in Georgia, South Carolina, and North Carolina, Ferguson was quite intent on tracking down the Overmountain Men on their own turf, so he sent a message to Colonel Isaac Shelby. Samuel Phillips, who served with Shelby, was a prisoner in Ferguson's control. Ferguson promised to parole Phillips if he would deliver a message to Shelby, indicating that if Shelby and the other backwater officers "did not desist from their opposition to the British arms, he would march his army over the mountains, hang their leaders, and lay their country waste with fire and sword."[92]

Phillips took the message directly to Shelby, along with information on Ferguson's location and the strength of his forces. Shelby, annoyed and provoked by the message, rode from Sapling Grove to Colonel John Sevier's home on the Nolachucky, where he found a crowd attending a horse race. Speaking privately, the two men spent two days in discussion, both agreeing that a surprise attack on the enemy was necessary before their settlements were invaded. They asked for the cooperation of militias commanded by Colonel William Campbell, who agreed to meet up with them on the southern Virginia border, traveling through Flower Gap. Lieutenant Colonel Sevier was also informed, and Shelby issued an order calling on all the militia of the county to be ready to march at the appointed time.[93]

Shelby had hoped that Campbell would meet them closer to the Watauga settlement, as they had been warned of another Cherokee attack. When Shelby explained his concerns, Campbell agreed to meet them at the

A glimpse of artist Richard Luce's painting of the muster of the Overmountain Men. The complete reproduced painting showcases the entrance to the Sycamore Shoals State Historic Park Museum. *Courtesy of Cory Franklin.*

determined meeting site. Concurrently, Sevier kept Colonels Charles McDowell and Andrew Hampton informed and equipped for the march. McDowell and Hampton had been at Colonel John Carter's since September 18 and were encamped on the Watauga.

People across the settlement were working hard and purposefully to prepare the militia for this important expedition. Failure was not an option. Mary Patton on Powder Branch began producing gunpower for the men at her powder mill. By September 25, she had produced about five hundred pounds of powder for the men, which was purchased from her by William Cobb. In addition, food was being gathered, Matthew Talbot's gristmill was grinding meal to bake bread, and a lead mine close to John Sevier's home near today's Bumpus Cove provided lead for musket balls.[94]

Currency and coin were not easily accessible west of the mountains, which had Shelby and Sevier struggling to find a way to purchase needed supplies. Sevier and possibly Shelby, meeting at McDowell's encampment on Watauga, made a proposal to John Adair, the entry taker for Sullivan County. They requested that the public funds in Adair's control—believed to have amounted to $12,000 to $13,000—be advanced to meet the supply need if war on the home front or beyond became reality. Adair explained he did not have the authority to make this type of disposition of the money, continuing,

> *It belongs to the impoverished treasury of North Carolina, and I dare not appropriate a cent of it to any other purpose; but if the country is overrun by the British our liberty is gone. Let the money go too. Take it. If the enemy, by its use, is driven from the country, I can trust that country to justify and vindicate my conduct—so take it.*

If the State of North Carolina demanded the money, Shelby and Sevier pledged to ensure its return. In 1782, Adair received an acquittance or receipt for these funds.[95]

With the preparations coming together, the place was set for the rendezvous of all militia commands to meet at the Sycamore Shoals or Flats of the Watauga River on September 25, 1780.[96]

A large amount of excitement and activity was evident: Women prepared their sons and husbands for their journey, beeves (beef) were gathered at the Shoals, and food for travel was prepared. John Sevier's new wife, Catherine Sherrill, made and repaired clothes for her husband and sons, as did the wives of many of the men preparing to muster.

Above: Food was prepared for travel along with clothing for the men who were to muster at Sycamore Shoals. *Courtesy of the author.*

Opposite: On September 25, 1780, the Overmountain Men mustered at Sycamore Shoals in preparation for their march in search of British Major Patrick Ferguson. *Courtesy of the author.*

Every man, young or old, wished to go, but some were not able, and others stayed behind, chosen by a reverse draft, to protect their families and the settlement from possible Cherokee attack. Colonel Anthony Bledsoe was left in command of Sullivan County and Major Charles Robertson in Washington County.

On September 25, at the Sycamore Shoals muster, volunteers and militia gathered in numbers higher than ever expected. Marching in search of Ferguson were 240 men under Lieutenant Colonel John Sevier of Washington County, North Carolina; 240 men under Colonel Isaac Shelby of Sullivan County, North Carolina; 200 under Colonel William Campbell of Washington County, Virginia; and 160 under Colonel Charles McDowell from Burke and Rutherford Counties, North Carolina, who were currently camped near Watauga after fleeing North Carolina. Colonel Arthur Campbell brought 400 men, who joined the ranks of Colonel William Campbell, while Arthur returned home to protect his county. Arthur McDowell also returned home to protect his counties against Native incursions.[97]

Left: Men of African descent, some free and some not, joined the Patriot cause. *Courtesy of Sycamore Shoals State Historic Park.*

Below: Children under sixteen, discovered in pension records, served as fifers, drummers, buglers, fighters, and more. *Courtesy of Sycamore Shoals State Historic Park.*

The larger part of those mustering were riflemen clothed in hunting shirts, carrying a shot pouch, a Deckard rifle, a tomahawk, a knife, a cup, a wallet of provisions such as parched corn, a knapsack, a blanket, and moccasins—all mostly made themselves. Some carried a skillet. Five men of African descent joined the Patriot army, included two freedmen, Esaius Bowman and Andrew Ferguson. Ishmael Titus, an enslaved man, earned his freedom by going in place of his master. John Broddy, Colonel William Campbell's body servant, also served. A third freedman of color, Primus, applied for a pension in 1846, claiming he fought in many battles, including Kings Mountain.

Pension records show that children age sixteen and under were present also, often as fifers, drummers, buglers, teamsters, spies, couriers, and scouts; some of them fought in battle. William Price and Presley Larkins, both age thirteen, are two known fifers; fifteen-year-old William Cross served as a drummer.

The enormity and energy of the people coming together at the muster was described by J.G.M. Ramsey, who, reflecting on the scenario stated, "Never did mountain recess contain within it a loftier or more enlarged patriotism—never a cooler or more determined courage."[98]

The morning of September 26, the Reverend Samuel Doak led the group in prayer and devotions before their journey. As he opened, his words reached the hearts of all: "My countrymen, you are about to set out on an expedition which is full of hardships and dangers, but one in which the Almighty will attend you." He then addressed their liberties, taxation without representation, the call for help from across the mountains, their experiences with war, and preventing the enemy from "bringing fire and sword to their very doors." His inspirational words and blessings on the militia were followed by prayer, ending with, "Help us as good soldiers to wield the Sword of the Lord and Gideon!"

Humbled and inspired, the overmountain militia said their goodbyes and began their travels up Gap Creek, later crossing to the Doe River. They reached the Shelving Rock in Roan Mountain, where they stored their black powder on the first night and encamped there. Blacksmith John Miller, who was living about a mile upriver, helped to shoe several of the men's horses.

The next day, the men were to cross the Yellow Mountains (possibly through Yellow Mountain Gap) at an elevation of 4,682 feet after camping at the Shelving Rock, at about 2,600 feet, climbing approximately 2,000 feet to cross into North Carolina. Realizing that the cattle were slowing them down, they left them behind. As they trekked up the mountain, they soon

Left: The Reverend Samuel Doak prayed with the Overmountain Men as they prepared to depart in search of Ferguson on September 26. *Courtesy of the author.*

Below: The Overmountain Men made their first camp after leaving Sycamore Shoals at the Shelving Rock in Roan Mountain. This image from the early to mid-1900s shows the Daughters of the American Revolution placing a plaque in honor of the Patriots of 1780. *Courtesy of the author.*

found themselves in "shoe-mouth-deep" snow. On reaching the bald of the Roan, the troops drilled and practiced firing their rifles.[99]

Along the journey, Sevier realized that two of his men were missing and suspected they might be Tories with a plan to warn Ferguson of the approaching army. Not wanting Ferguson to find them, the men changed their route. They descended from Yellow Mountain and moved on to Gillespie Gap and then divided the commands into two groups that would come together at Quaker Meadows. There, Colonels Benjamin Cleveland and Winston met up with them along with an additional 350 men and Colonel Arthur Campbell with 200 men; other volunteers joined them en route.[100]

Expecting to find Ferguson at Gilbert Town, they encamped about eighteen miles outside that town on October 2 with about 1,500 men. With no commanding officer assigned, differences and arguments among this large group of volunteers started to become a problem. First, a request was sent to Horatio Gates to provide a commanding officer, but he did not respond. Colonel William Campbell from Virginia was then recommended by Shelby; all the officers supported his choice.

By now, the two deserters had caught up with Ferguson who, after hearing their message, left Gilbert Town with a smaller force and headed south to address Cornwallis. At Denard's Ford, Ferguson began soliciting for Tories to join his army. His solicitation notice referred to the Overmountain Men as "barbarians," "murderers," and the "dregs of mankind." Ferguson's use of words to encourage Loyalists to join his army culminated with: "If you choose to be 'degraded' by a set of mongrels, say so at once, and let your women turn their backs upon you, and look out for real men to protect them." His sales pitch seemed to accomplish the task at hand, bringing in several hundred more men to join his ranks.[101]

Meanwhile, Colonels Cleveland and Shelby were addressing their men at Cane Creek in Morganton, North Carolina, on how to engage in battle with their enemy. Shelby told them,

> *When you encounter the enemy, don't wait for the word of command. Let each one of you be his own officer, taking every care, you can of yourselves.... If in the woods, shelter yourselves and give them Indian play! Advance from tree to tree, pressing the enemy and killing and disabling all you can.*

On October 6, the overmountain militia made it to Cowpens, an estate they took over from its Tory owner, eating well on his cattle and corn. Sometime after, they sent out a fellow named Gilmer to try to get information on

Ferguson's location by pretending he wanted to join him. He was successful in learning where Ferguson was heading, the strength of his army, and how he communicated with Cornwallis.

Ferguson and eight hundred to one thousand men arrived at Kings Mountain, just across the North Carolina line in York County, South Carolina, on October 6, 1780. Ferguson marched his men up to the mountain's narrow bald top, lined with many rocks and boulders, where they pitched their tents. As evening drew near, Ferguson is said to have announced to his troops that he was on Kings Mountain, he was the king of that mountain, and God Almighty could not drive him from it.

Unbeknownst to Ferguson, Campbell and his officers were not far off and had with them over nine hundred of their best men, who had traveled overnight in rain and mud. Keeping their weapons and powder dry before themselves, the men did not stop until they were about two miles from Kings Mountain. There, they captured a messenger Ferguson had sent to request help. The messenger told them they would recognize Ferguson by his checked shirt or the duster he wore over his uniform.

As they approached their destination, the Patriot militia was led by Colonel William Campbell, who also led the Washington County Regiment of Militia from Virginia. Those following his orders were Colonel James Williams and the Little River District Regiment of Militia from South Carolina; Major Joseph McDowell and the Burke County Regiment of Militia from North Carolina; and Lieutenant Colonel John Sevier of the Washington County Regiment of Militia of North Carolina. Serving under these leaders were several militia units from the southeastern colonies.

On the afternoon of October 7, the rain ended by the time the militia reached Kings Mountain. The battle plan was to surround the mountain, keep the enemy on the top, and continue firing while hiding behind rocks and trees. Giving the militiamen the opportunity to back out before engaging the enemy, Shelby asked those who wished to leave to "march three steps to the rear." To Shelby's pleasure, not a man stepped back.[102]

As the battle commenced, Shelby's men found themselves in the line of opening fire and wished to return fire, but they were ordered to wait and to press on so their "fire will not be lost." When the men reached their places, Shelby called out, "Here they are boys! Shoot like hell and fight like the devils!" One can only imagine how unnerving the savage yells must have sounded to Ferguson and his men. Captain DePeyster recalled the yelling from another engagement and declared, "These are the same yelling devils that were at Musgrove Mill!"[103]

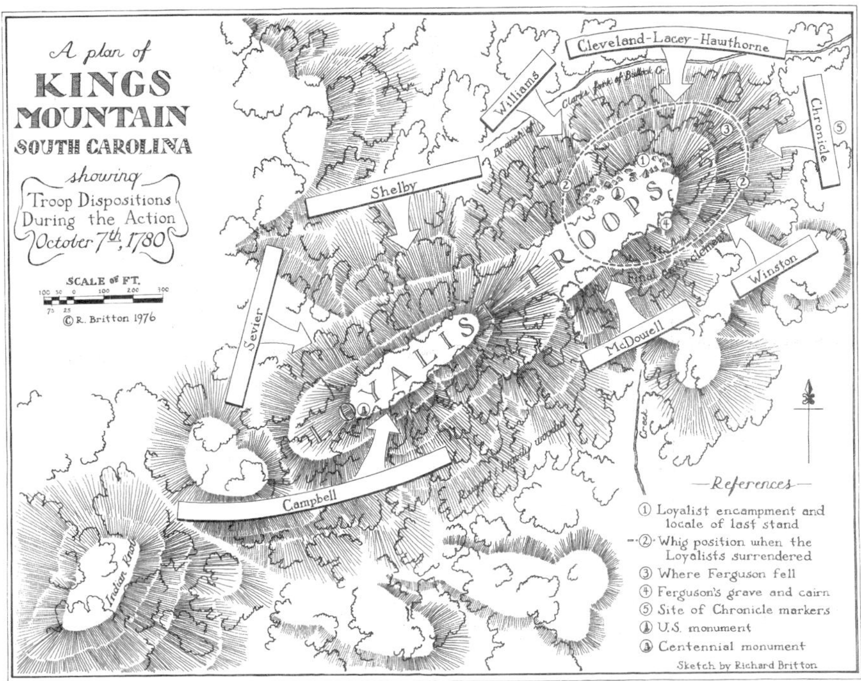

This map shows the positions of the troops on October 7, 1780, at Kings Mountain, South Carolina. *Courtesy of Sycamore Shoals State Historic Park.*

Cleveland moved among his men as they fought, encouraging and keeping them locked in on their mission, shouting, "Fire as quick as you can; stand your ground as long as you can." Shelby, on the side of the mountain, had begun leading his men across a gap in the forest when an alarm was sounded indicating the enemy was about to charge. The alarm came from Ferguson, who jumped onto his horse and began blowing his silver whistle, the command for his men to charge. Some did, only to be shot by Americans behind them.[104]

For a moment, the frontiersmen backed off, but Campbell commanded them to return to the fight. They began their climb again, moving from rock to tree. With sword in hand, Campbell continued forward, his men following on foot.

The Tory militia fell into disorder as the Overmountain Men continued their attack from all sides of the mountain. The circle of rebels was drawing in on Ferguson from all directions. Then Shelby and Sevier, leading their men, made it to the summit. Some of Ferguson's officers urged him to surrender, but he refused. Instead, he charged the Wataugans with his horse, swinging his sword.

Robert Young heard his son-in-law John Gilliland pull his trigger on spotting Ferguson, but his gun did not fire. Young, noting the misfire, aimed at Ferguson, saying, "I'll try and see what Sweet Lips can do," and fired the shot that many believe killed Ferguson. As Ferguson fell from his saddle, his foot was caught in a stirrup, and his body was dragged around the American troops. Some took a few extra shots at him, resulting in Ferguson receiving up to eight bullet wounds, one in his head. Some of those bullet wounds may have occurred after his death.[105]

With a drive to succeed like no other, the Overmountain Men, the "yelling boys," had defeated Ferguson in what has been reported as ranging from forty minutes to one hour and five minutes.[106] Captain DePeyster took command for a short time and then raised the white flag—among many white flags seen across the mountain—and surrendered his sword to Campbell. That night, the Americans and others spent the night, exhausted, on the battlefield, the mournful sounds of the wounded and the dying echoing in the background.

S.C. Williams writes that the American colonels reported that their forces numbered 1,187, based on the daily returns for rations. Colonel Ferguson's forces were estimated at about 1,400 men based on information provided by an officer to General Davidson three days later. Provision returns found in their camp indicated a force of 1,125 men. Reports of the number of men killed, wounded, and taken prisoner—both British and American—varied, though all sources reported a higher number of losses in the British forces.[107]

While accounting for the injured and the dead in both the British and American forces, several of the officers engaged in dividing Ferguson's belongings, consisting in part of his pistol, china, a silver whistle and watch, his sash and commission, and DePeyster's sword.[108]

After the battle, Colonel John Sevier sent Andrew Greer's twenty-year-old son, Joseph Greer, from Kings Mountain to the United States Congress, then assembled in Philadelphia, to share the news of the success of the Battle of Kings Mountain. Sevier believed that Joseph's understanding of the Indigenous people, acquired from joining his father when he traded with them, would give him an advantage as he traveled a long distance on his own. His trip was fraught with danger—he was shot at and tracked—but ended with his safe arrival in Philadelphia. When he arrived at congressional headquarters, he was not permitted entrance and pushed the guard aside so he could deliver his message from Sevier. On hearing the message, George Washington commented, "With soldiers like him, no wonder the frontiersmen won." Later, for his military service, Joseph received a three-thousand-acre grant in today's Lincoln County, Tennessee.[109]

In *Kings Mountain and Its Heroes*, Lyman Draper documents comments made by survivors the night after the battle. The scene was described by survivor Thomas Young as "awful, indeed," and a "dreadful day." Benjamin Sharp, in his narrative in the *American Pioneer*, wrote, "We had to encamp on the ground with the dead and wounded, and pass the night amid groans and lamentations."

At first light on the day after the battle, the men worked quickly to leave Kings Mountain as soon as possible. Before departing, they buried their deceased friends and burned wagons and anything that would slow their journey home. A casual jaunt was not in their plans as running up on Banastre Tarleton was an altercation they wanted to avoid.

Colonel Benjamin Cleveland rode out on Ferguson's white horse as his own horse had been killed, but as the victorious troops started their march home at midday, some of his men remained behind. They stayed for a short time so their prisoners could bury their dead and prepare cloth so the wounded could be removed with them, which greatly slowed down their progress.

As the overmountain militia began their march into North Carolina, they soon realized how hungry and exhausted they were from carrying guns and those wounded on litters. They stopped at the home of Aaron Bickerstaff, a Loyalist who died at Kings Mountain, gathering pumpkins, which they sliced and fried to help stave off their hunger. Some of the Carolina colonels suggested that Tories who had executed various outrages against the Patriots and their families be held accountable and court-martialed. Campbell called a court to order, resulting in thirty-some Tories being condemned to death by hanging. The precedent for this had been set earlier by Cornwallis, who had ordered the hanging of many rebels.[110]

After nine men were hanged from a large oak near the road, the younger brother of Isaac Baldwin, who was in the next group, threw himself on Isaac, crying. In his show of emotion, he was cutting the cords that bound Isaac, enabling him to escape. He was not stopped but was caught later. The court had begun to move on to hang the next three men when Colonel Shelby called a stop to the hangings and released and pardoned the remaining men. The remaining prisoners were taken to the prison at Hillsborough and were later released at the end of the revolution.[111]

Despite exhaustion, they were concerned they might encounter Tarleton, which made continuing their journey home a top priority. After crossing the Catawba River, they stayed at McDowell's estate at Quaker Meadows for a few days and then continued toward their homes.[112]

What the militia officers did not yet know was what the British response had been to their defeat of Ferguson and his militia at Kings Mountain. It wasn't long before the Patriots learned that Cornwallis had abandoned his plan to invade North Carolina and that Cornwallis and Tarleton were now in retreat to Winnsboro, South Carolina.[113]

On returning to the western waters, the frontier militia learned of threats against their homes and families by the Cherokee and Chickamauga that were instigated by General Cornwallis. Cornwallis, writing to General Henry Clinton, stated,

> *When the numerous and formidable bodies of back mountain-men came down to attack Major Ferguson and showed themselves to be our inveterate enemies, I directed Lieutenant Colonel Brown to encourage the Indians to attack the settlements of Watauga, Holston, Caentuck* [Kentucky] *and Nolachuckie....A large body of the mountaineers were soon obliged to oppose the* [British-incited] *incursions of the Indians.*

Cornwallis's letter inspired up to 2,500 Cherokee to attack the settlements in retribution for the Kings Mountain attack over the winter—if provided with arms, ammunition, and clothing for their families.[114]

The western settlements had little choice but to defend themselves and their families. On December 16, 1780, at the Battle of Boyd's Creek, Colonels Sevier, Campbell, Martin, and Clark with a seven-hundred-man militia engaged the Cherokee. Boyd's Creek is considered the only Revolutionary War battle in today's state of Tennessee. The militia continued to the Cherokee towns of Chota and Coyatee on the Little Tennessee River, which they destroyed after the Cherokee's British-supported attack on the western settlements.

Word of the Patriot success at Kings Mountain began to spread, and many leaders offered positive accolades. General Horatio Gates found the victory "great and glorious," while General George Washington said the win was "a proof of the spirit and resources of the country." The Continental Congress complimented Colonel Campbell's troops for "spirited and military conduct." Those fighting for the Patriot cause had reason to feel hopeful that their efforts could result in independence, while the Loyalists may have been concerned by the apparent retreat of Cornwallis and change in strategy. Later, in 1822, Thomas Jefferson, reflecting on the Kings Mountain victory, wrote that it was the "joyful annunciation of that turn of the tide of success, which terminated the Revolutionary War with the seal of independence."

The American Revolutionary war did not end immediately after the Kings Mountain battle. Provoked by Cornwallis, conflicts between settlers west of the mountains and the Cherokee and Chickamauga continued as the Native tribes had been encouraged by the British to attack the settlers.

Just three months after Kings Mountain, General Daniel Morgan's Patriot force defeated Colonel Banastre Tarleton on January 17, 1781, at the Battle of Cowpens near Chesnee, South Carolina, in a battle that lasted less than an hour.

After Cowpens, Lord Cornwallis, stationed in Winnsborough, South Carolina, had plans to again try to take control of North Carolina. General Nathanael Greene reached out to Isaac Shelby and John Sevier, who had just returned from the Cherokee wars, to see if either would take a command to protect North Carolina, but neither could accept at that time. Sevier put Major Charles Robertson to the task of leading a battalion to assist Greene. Robertson assembled a force of 130 men and began their march in late February 1781, reaching Greene's army around March 6. Colonel William Campbell, expected to bring 1,000 men, arrived with just 60 riflemen.

Greene and Campbell's forces engaged in skirmishes before both meeting up with Cornwallis's army on March 15, 1781, near Guilford Courthouse, where 85 percent of Greene's army engaged with Cornwallis's army for the first time. Greene's army outnumbered Cornwallis's, but as Cornwallis advanced, Greene sounded a retreat, resulting in much confusion as his men stampeded to the rear, leaving the battlefield. This resulted in the British splitting the American army into two sections with the Americans to their rear and Campbell's men on their flanks. Ultimately the battle ended with a British victory. Cornwallis lost 25 percent of his troops in a battle referred to as "one of the bloodiest of the war." After this engagement, Cornwallis moved his troops to the coast of Wilmington, North Carolina, to rest and prepare to continue their campaign to control North Carolina.[115]

General Greene's focus was on reducing the British presence and forts in Georgia and South Carolina. Ninety-Six was the only fort left in South Carolina, so Greene wrote to Shelby indicating his need for reinforcements to accomplish this mission. Shelby, who was engaged in treaty negotiations with the Cherokee, could not leave until around July 15. Shelby and his men did not arrive at Ninety-Six as hoped for, but on August 3, Shelby wrote to General Greene that the treaty was completed on July 29 and he was planning to send reinforcements and had learned that the enemy had retreated to Orangeburg and maybe Charlestown. Due to the distance, Shelby and other forces from the western settlements held their men in readiness for when they were needed.

Greene continued, engaging with the British at the Battle of Eutaw Springs on September 8 and emerging victorious. On September 16, he wrote to Shelby informing him of the battle and of Cornwallis having been pushed toward Charlestown, along with news of a French fleet of at least thirty ships arriving in the Chesapeake Bay. On September 16, Greene pleaded in a letter for Shelby to march riflemen to Charlotte to join other forces. Sevier and Shelby saw the importance of the call and enlisted volunteers who also saw the need to intercept Lord Cornwallis and possibly end the war in the south.[116]

While Sevier and Shelby continued their march through North Carolina, word came that Cornwallis had surrendered his eight-thousand-man army to General George Washington and the Continental army and their French allies, under General Comte de Rochambeau, at Yorktown, Virginia on October 19, 1781. The Siege of Yorktown, the last major battle of the war, began on September 18, 1781; the British were outnumbered and outfought during the three-week siege.[117]

The Overmountain Men continued on and rendezvoused with Francis Marion, the Swamp Fox, where there was ample forage to feed their horses. Shelby was reluctant to accept this assignment as his men would be seventy to eighty miles farther from their homes.

Shelby and Sevier's troops served their sixty days and did not arrive home until early January 1782. Toward the end of their service, they encountered and engaged with Hessians and other men of the British army who were without leadership following Cornwallis's surrender.

Shelby, in describing his troops, wrote, "These mountaineers were poor men who lived by keeping stock on the range beyond the mountains; they were volunteers and neither expected or received any compensation except liquidated certificates worth two shillings in the pound."[118] John Haywood's words supported Shelby's: "To the honor of the troops under Sevier and Shelby, no…captive negroes or property came with them into the counties of their residence; their integrity was as little impeached as their valor." Haywood was comparing the mountain men's conduct to the looting practiced by some Tories and the theft of African Americans sold into slavery.[119]

The August 19, 1782 Battle of Blue Licks, near the Licking River in Kentucky, was fought ten months after Lord Cornwallis surrendered at Yorktown and is considered the last major battle of the Revolutionary War

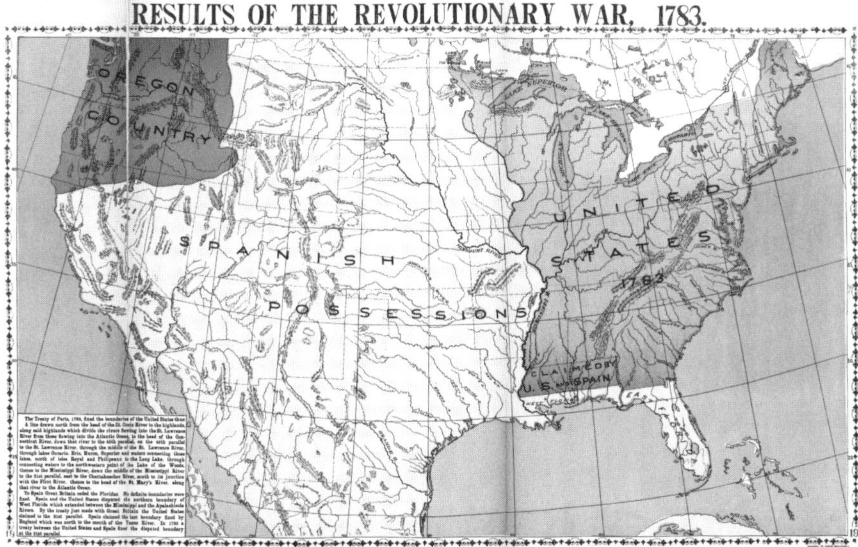

Above: This map, "Results of the Revolutionary War in 1783," indicates land ownership at the time. *Library of Congress, Geography and Map Division.*

Left: In 1938, the Daughters of the American Revolution placed a monument on G Street in Elizabethton honoring the Overmountain Men and Watauga settlers. *Courtesy of Sycamore Shoals State Historic Park.*

west of the Appalachian Mountains. The Kentucky militia was ambushed by British Loyalists and Native forces under Captain William Caldwell, whose goal was British control of the western frontier. The battle ended with the defeat of the Kentucky militiamen and heavy casualties.

American Revolutionary War peace negotiations took place at the Treaty of Paris in 1783, in which Britian acknowledged the sovereignty and independence of the United States. The treaty was signed on September 3, 1783, ending the war that began on March 22, 1775, with the British implementation of the Stamp Act. Boundaries were established, among other business decisions involving property, war debt, fishing rights, and navigation on the Mississippi River.

Britain formally recognized the United States of America as a sovereign, independent, and free nation, and the United States Confederation Congress ratified the treaty on January 14, 1784, in Annapolis, Maryland.

Chapter 9

BECOMING TENNESSEE

The State of Franklin and the Southwest Territory

The State of Franklin

By the end of the Revolutionary War in 1783, Washington County, created in 1777, and Sullivan County, created in 1779, were both well established. Greene County, established in 1782, had a growing population. Others were moving into the Cumberland country by way of a new road, begun in 1784, between Long Island of the Holston and the French Lick, today's Nashville, Tennessee. After years of war and conflict between the colonies and the British, along with the Cherokee and Chickamauga, it seemed that peace could become a part of everyone's lives.

To alleviate the financial burden created during the war, in 1784, the North Carolina legislature passed the Cession Act, which enabled the state to transfer its western lands, in addition to the Watauga settlements, to the United States Congress. The same year, the Continental Congress passed the Land Ordinance of 1784, calling for western lands to be ceded to the government so they might be divided into ten states, which would later be admitted to the Union. With no Congressional plan or constitution yet in place to form a territorial government or to create new states, the civil leadership of the counties from the Washington District decided it was in their best interest to make their own state.

After two constitutional conventions were held in Jonesborough, a temporary constitution was framed and adopted on December 14, 1784.

At the second convention, Reverend Samuel Houston presented the State of Frankland Constitution, which was rejected. John Sevier then suggested revising the constitution of the State of North Carolina to suit their needs, which was approved November 14, 1785. It included a declaration of independence and support for the new state of Frankland's actions, ending with: "5th and Lastly. We unanimously agree that our lives, liberties and property can be more secure, and our happiness much better propagated by our separation; and consequently, that it is our duty and inalienable right to form ourselves into a new and independent State."[120]

The proposed new state was named Frankland, which included Greene, Sullivan, and Washington Counties. John Sevier was elected governor, F.A. Ramsey secretary, Landon Carter speaker, Thomas Talbot clerk of the senate, William Cage speaker, and Thomas Chapman, clerk of the house of commons.

A delegation, represented by William Cocke, submitted a petition on May 16, 1785, asking that Frankland be admitted to the Union as a new and separate state. The Congressional committee's response was favorable, and the petition was presented to the full body for a vote. Seven states voted in favor of receiving Franklin, two voted against, and two states were absent from the vote, but the required two-thirds majority did not happen.

Governor Martin of Virginia was not in favor of statehood for Frankland, commenting that if anyone in his state tried to form a new government, they would be tried for high treason. Martin also intended to maintain North Carolina's jurisdiction in all parts of the state—by force if necessary. The Continental Congress would not act favorably without the support of North Carolina, which was also against accepting Frankland. North Carolina had plans to take back the lands they had ceded to Congress. North Carolina's lack of approval was the virtual nail in the coffin. Lacking a two-thirds majority, Frankland did not become the fourteenth state in the new Union. Later in 1785, the name of Frankland was changed to Franklin, in hopes of getting the support of Benjamin Franklin, which did not come to pass.[121]

Ultimately, divided loyalties formed between two sets of representatives: one representing North Carolina, referred to as the Tiptonites, led by Captain John Tipton, and one for the state of Frankland, referred to as the Franklinites, led by Governor John Sevier. Tipton had supported Houston's constitution but did not support the constitution patterned after North Carolina's. The disagreements between Sevier and Tipton resulted in ongoing altercations between the two groups.

Hoping to end the conflicts and regain the allegiance of the western settlement citizens, North Carolina extended the 1783 Act of Pardon and Oblivion in 1788. The 1783 act offered amnesty and the restoration of citizenship to those accused of crimes during the Revolutionary War. In 1788, North Carolina extended the 1783 act to the Franklin region, providing pardons to those who participated in the formation of the state of Franklin. To reap the benefits of the act, an individual would also have to take an oath of allegiance to the State of North Carolina.[122]

In early 1788, a North Carolina court issued an order to satisfy a judgement against John Sevier. It was given to Washington County Sheriff Jonathan Pugh, who was ordered to seize Sevier's property. Pugh levied it on Sevier's enslaved people to satisfy the judgement and took them to the home of Colonel John Tipton for safekeeping.[123]

Sevier believed these actions were unlawful as they violated the Franklin Act of March 1787, which called for punishment of those performing official acts under the laws of North Carolina. Sevier raised a force of about 150 men, planning to march to Tipton's on February 27, 1788, to end the raids on and opposition to the Frankland courts and reclaim his illegally removed enslaved people. Here began the Battle of the State of Franklin.[124]

On their arrival, a demand was sent to Tipton asking for his surrender within thirty minutes and his submission to the laws of Franklin. Tipton did not respond; therefore, conflict continued through the next day. When Sevier sent another request to surrender, Tipton's response indicated his intention to abide by the laws of North Carolina. Then, on the morning of February 29, a heavy snowstorm set in, preventing Sevier's men from noticing the arrival of men coming to assist Tipton. A ten-minute fight ensued, in which three men were killed and several captured or wounded on both sides. Sevier and his men retreated, with Tipton in pursuit. Robert Young Jr. intercepted the Tiptonites, requesting that Sevier be given time to consider terms. Tipton responded with a date: March 11.

Sevier held council and then, on March 3, sent the state of Franklin council's decision to Tipton. The expiration of Sevier's term as governor fell within days of the battle. His term expired on March 1, and his chosen successor, General Evan Shelby, was not interested in the nomination. Without leadership, Franklin could not function without a governor or a judge.

The council of Franklin then indicated to John Tipton that it wanted peace, though it did not intend to support North Carolina. As time passed,

The Battle of the State of Franklin, illustration by John Alan Maxwell. *Courtesy of Tipton Haynes State Historic Site.*

others, who remained strong supporters of Sevier, began leaving the Franklin movement and aligning themselves politically with North Carolina.[125]

In July 1788, North Carolina Governor Johnston ordered the arrest of Sevier on charges of treason against the State of North Carolina. In October, Sevier was visiting Jonesborough when word of his presence at Jacob Brown's widow's home reached John Tipton. Tipton, with ten men, found and arrested Sevier. He was to be held in the Jonesborough jail, but to prevent a possible rescue and bloodshed, he was moved to Morganton, North Carolina. When Sevier arrived in Burke County, word got to Colonel Charles McDowell and Major Joseph McDowell of his arrest. They went with the prisoner to Morganton and stepped in and became sureties on his bail bond. Soon after, a group of relatives and friends of Sevier arrived in Morganton, planning to rescue him. Arriving at a tavern, they found Sevier there with the McDowells. Sevier soon left and headed back home with his friends and family.[126]

At the Greene County Court in February 1789, John Sevier, Joseph Hardin, Henry Conway, and Hugh Wear "came into court and took the oath of allegiance, agreeable to the Act of the Assembly in such cases made and provided." Up until this point, these men had not given up on their dream of a state of Frankland. Taking the oath was a commitment of their future intentions. Samuel Cole Williams, in *The Lost State of Franklin*, states, "This action officially ended the State of Franklin."[127]

There is a second school of thought on when the state of Frankland ended. Many contend that when John Sevier's term as governor ended on March 1, 1788, after the Battle of the State of Franklin, the organization ceased to exist, as no one was willing to step up into a leadership position.

Whatever the case may be, the state of Franklin did come to an end, and all citizens were expected to adhere to the laws of North Carolina. In due time, the Territory South of the River Ohio came to be on May 26, 1790.

Today, Tipton Haynes State Historic Site in Johnson City, Tennessee, is operated in partnership with the Tennessee Historical Commission and the Tipton-Haynes Historical Association. The forty-five-acre site features eleven historic buildings, the Tipton/Gifford/Simerly cemetery, a limestone cave, a natural spring, a buffalo trace, and a nature trail. The visitor center includes a museum store, educational spaces, a library, archives, and a permanent interpretive exhibit.

The Southwest Territory

The cession of North Carolina's western territory to the federal government was at last accepted by Congress on April 2, 1790, via "An Act to Accept a Cession of the Claims of the State of North Carolina to a Certain District of Western Territory." The act provided a means by which North Carolina could pay its debt to the federal government. Additionally, it provided for a military reservation "for the benefit of the officers and soldiers of the continental line of North Carolina." It also allowed the federal government to control western lands and gave it the ability to establish a more unified nation—for instance, by determining how those lands would be broken up into separate states.[128]

The Territory South of the River Ohio, also known as the Southwest Territory, was created on May 26, 1790. On June 8, William Blount was commissioned by President Washington as governor of this territory. Daniel Smith served as secretary along with Brigadier Generals John Sevier of the Washington District militia and James Robertson of the Mero District militia.[129]

Rocky Mount became the first territorial capital of the Southwest Territory and was divided into two districts: the Washington District, including lands north of the French Broad River and northeast of the meeting of the Clinch and Tennessee Rivers, and the Mero District, taking in lands near today's Nashville north to the border of Kentucky. The two districts were connected by Avery's Trace, a road that traversed the lands of Indigenous people.

The existing counties of Washington, Sullivan, Hawkins and Greene, created by North Carolina, became part of the Washington District. Davidson, Sumner, and Tennessee Counties joined the Mero District. In 1792, Blount added the counties of Knox and Jefferson to the territory. The Southwest Territory was well on its way to meeting the minimum number of citizens to qualify for statehood.

Since 1770, William Cobb had made Rocky Mount, where he built a two-story log house, his home. William's family supported their community, and when the call to muster came in 1780, William, William Jr., Pharaoh, Jerry, and Arthur Cobb all volunteered to march in search of Patrick Ferguson.

In 1790, when Governor Blount arrived at the home of William Cobb in Washington County, "it became at once the seat of the territorial government and remained so until the spring of 1792 when the governor would move to

The William Cobb homeplace at Rocky Mount State Historic Site. *Courtesy of Rebecca Moriarity Smith.*

Knoxville, a town yet to be laid out at James White's fort, 105 miles to the southwest." Blount began construction of his mansion in October 1791, and his family arrived at Rocky Mount in December 1791.[130]

With the British out of the picture, the Cherokee towns of Running Water, Nickajack, Long Island Villages, Crow Town, and Lockout Mountain continued taking hostile action toward the white settlers early in 1792. Little Turkey, principal chief of the Cherokee, did not support the actions of these five towns and thus forbade the members of his nation to interact with them.[131]

By the end of 1792 and continuing into 1793, the hostilities of the Chickamauga had become never-ending in the Southwest Territory and the Cumberland settlements. In other parts of the United States, other tribes were also engaged in warfare. To those living amid these threats, it appeared that the federal government was either not aware or not engaged with the problem.

Before the closing of 1792, the state capitol was established in Knoxville, Tennessee. Governor Blount's assembly consisted of an elected house of representatives and a territorial council appointed by the president of the United States. In February 1794, the assembly met in Knoxville. They discussed the need to protect the frontier people, writing and approving an address to Congress. The assembly demanded that war be declared against the Creek and Cherokee, justified by the killing of up to two hundred citizens of all ages in a "barbarous and inhuman manner," including theft, taking captives, and destroying property and crops.[132]

As Native raids and new hostilities grew in numbers throughout the settlements in 1794, the federal government refused to change its policy. The governor's request regarding support in conducting offensive operations was denied. Secretary Knox, commenting on the denied request to strike Chickamauga towns, wrote on July 26, "I am instructed…by the President, to say, that he does not conceive himself authorized to direct any such measure." Knox went on to state that Congress did not find it proper to authorize or direct offensive operations.[133]

On November 8, 1794, Governor Blount, key chiefs and about five hundred warriors met at the Tellico Blockhouse, a United States fort in today's Vonore, Tennessee, built to protect the Cherokee from encroaching settlers. The purpose of the meeting was to discuss peace, resulting in the Treaty of the Tellico Blockhouse between the United States and Cherokee. It ended the Chickamauga wars and reinstated boundaries associated with the Holston Treaty. The parties to the treaty agreed to a future prisoner exchange. Furthermore, Blount asked the Cherokee to prevent the Creek from crossing their lands to attack the settlements. The Cherokee agreed and indicated they would not assist the Creek.

On June 1–3, 1795, the parties met again for a partial exchange of prisoners, and the Cherokee again pledged that their nation would strive for peace with the settlers. In striving for good relations with the Cherokee, Blount ordered the "removal of United States citizens who had settled on Cherokee lands in Powell's Valley in violation of the Treaty of the Holston." His words were well intentioned, but there are doubts that anyone actually moved as there are no records indicating that they did so.[134]

The territorial general assembly, interested in pursuing statehood, met in Knoxville in January 1795 at the request of Governor Blount. The assembly voted to take a population census and voted on whether to seek statehood. Only one representative was against. According to the statehood census taken in late November into December 1795, the population was 77,262, well above the 60,000-citizen requirement.

In April 1796, prior to admission to the Union, Carter County became the first county established by the first general assembly of Tennessee. Carter County was named for Landon Carter, the son of John Carter, and was created from parts of Washington County, the oldest in the state, and all of present-day Johnson County. The town of Elizabethton was founded in 1799 and named after Landon's wife, Elizabeth.[135]

After the proposed state of Tennessee adopted its constitution and elected officials, it petitioned Congress for statehood. The State of Tennessee was ratified on June 1, 1796, becoming the sixteenth state to join the Union.[136]

Rocky Mount State Historic Site in Piney Flats, Tennessee, operates in partnership with the Tennessee Historical Commission and the Rocky Mount Historical Association. Historic structures, an interpretive museum, an auditorium, and a gift shop add to the visitor's experience. Tours and interpretive programs are offered throughout the year.

Chapter 10

SYCAMORE SHOALS TODAY

In 1964, the land encompassing Sycamore Shoals was designated a national historic landmark through the support of Stewart Udall, secretary of the interior under the Kennedy administration. In 1966, it was placed on the National Register of Historic Places.

Sycamore Shoals State Historic Park received a second national historic landmark designation in 1975 from the National Park Service and United States Department of the Interior for having national significance in commemorating the history of the United States of America. It became a part of the Tennessee State Park system during the nation's bicentennial and was dedicated on July 2, 1976.

Events included a performance by the Betsytowne Fife and Drum Corps, led by Ken Northmore, and special recognition of Judge Ben Allen for his never-wavering dedication, vision, drive, and being the inspiration behind a goal that was now coming to fruition. Governor Ray Blanton and Commissioner of Conservation B.R. Allison attended as guests of honor; Blanton emphasized that "every American can take pride in Sycamore Shoals." The ribbon was cut, and to this day, Sycamore Shoals stays true to its mission of preservation and protection along with inspiring others by sharing its remarkable stories.

As you read on, you will find that events and organizations that have influenced the growth and changes the park has seen since its beginning are highlighted.

The Watauga Historical Association

Before 1962, area citizens and leaders saw the need to protect Sycamore Shoals and hoped to do so by having it designated a Tennessee state park. Generating state support for a new park did not happen overnight but came to pass as a host of dedicated local supporters worked tirelessly to make others aware of its significance. They raised funds and garnered support from the community, the state, and community leadership. A committee was soon formed, whose primary goal was to acquire and protect these historic lands and history through state ownership.

Efforts began to create a corporation focused on the Sycamore Shoals project. Judge Ben Allen, the Carter County chairman of the Tennessee American Revolution Bicentennial Commission, took a leading role and was admired for his active involvement from start to finish. Later, at the dedication of the new state park, he saw everyone's dream come to fruition before his death on March 20, 1977. The association honored him as its founder and its first president.

The committee first met with the Tennessee Historical Commission, which encouraged them to create a local organization for the purpose of supporting the acquisition of the lands surrounding Sycamore Shoals. The organization was called the Watauga Historical Association, whose incorporators first met at the University of Tennessee Law School building in Knoxville, Tennessee, on October 20, 1962, after filing their corporate charter on October 15, 1962. The incorporators included the first chairman of the board, Governor

Left: Sycamore Shoals of the Watauga River in 1938. *Courtesy of Sycamore Shoals State Historic Park.*

Opposite: The 1962 Charter of the Watauga Historic Association. *Courtesy of Sycamore Shoals State Historic Park.*

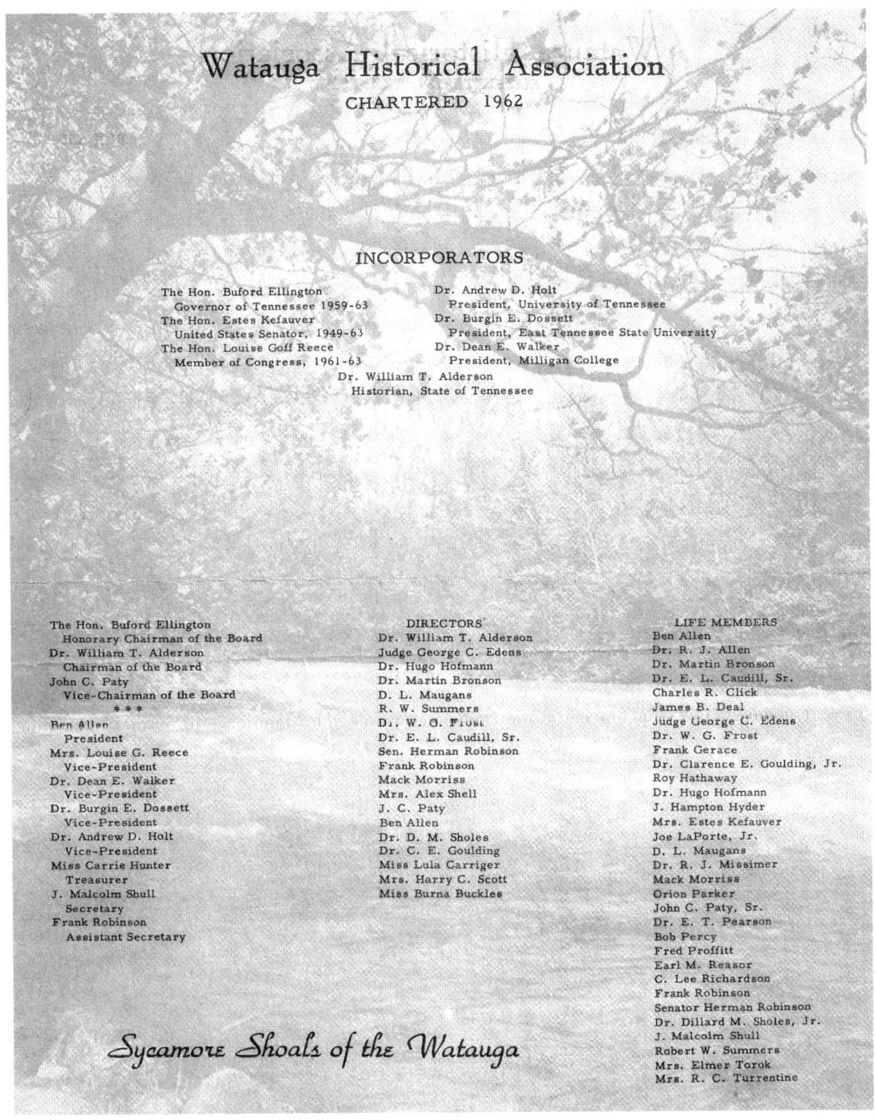

Watauga Historical Association

CHARTERED 1962

INCORPORATORS

The Hon. Buford Ellington
Governor of Tennessee 1959-63
The Hon. Estes Kefauver
United States Senator, 1949-63
The Hon. Louise Goff Reece
Member of Congress, 1961-63

Dr. Andrew D. Holt
President, University of Tennessee
Dr. Burgin E. Dossett
President, East Tennessee State University
Dr. Dean E. Walker
President, Milligan College

Dr. William T. Alderson
Historian, State of Tennessee

The Hon. Buford Ellington
Honorary Chairman of the Board
Dr. William T. Alderson
Chairman of the Board
John C. Paty
Vice-Chairman of the Board
* * *
Ben Allen
President
Mrs. Louise G. Reece
Vice-President
Dr. Dean E. Walker
Vice-President
Dr. Burgin E. Dossett
Vice-President
Dr. Andrew D. Holt
Vice-President
Miss Carrie Hunter
Treasurer
J. Malcolm Shull
Secretary
Frank Robinson
Assistant Secretary

DIRECTORS
Dr. William T. Alderson
Judge George C. Edens
Dr. Hugo Hofmann
Dr. Martin Bronson
D. L. Maugans
R. W. Summers
Dr. W. G. Frost
Dr. E. L. Caudill, Sr.
Sen. Herman Robinson
Frank Robinson
Mack Morriss
Mrs. Alex Shell
J. C. Paty
Ben Allen
Dr. D. M. Sholes
Dr. C. E. Goulding
Miss Lula Carriger
Mrs. Harry C. Scott
Miss Burna Buckles

LIFE MEMBERS
Ben Allen
Dr. R. J. Allen
Dr. Martin Bronson
Dr. E. L. Caudill, Sr.
Charles R. Click
James B. Deal
Judge George C. Edens
Dr. W. G. Frost
Frank Gerace
Dr. Clarence E. Goulding, Jr.
Roy Hathaway
Dr. Hugo Hofmann
J. Hampton Hyder
Mrs. Estes Kefauver
Joe LaPorte, Jr.
D. L. Maugans
Dr. R. J. Missimer
Mack Morriss
Orion Parker
John C. Paty, Sr.
Dr. E. T. Pearson
Bob Percy
Fred Proffitt
Earl M. Reasor
C. Lee Richardson
Frank Robinson
Senator Herman Robinson
Dr. Dillard M. Sholes, Jr.
J. Malcolm Shull
Robert W. Summers
Mrs. Elmer Torok
Mrs. R. C. Turrentine

Sycamore Shoals of the Watauga

Buford Ellington, and officers Senator Estes Kefauver, Representative Louise G. Reece, Dr. Andrew D. Holt; Dr. Burgin E. Dossett, Dr. Dean Walker, and Dr. William T. Alderson.

In 1963, association members flew to Washington, D.C., to meet with Secretary of the Interior Stewart Udall. His department provided the help of National Park Service planners to produce a basic design for the development of Sycamore Shoals.

The association quickly got to work acquiring acreage. The initial purchase of 6.9 acres was made through contributions of $7,500 from local citizens. In March 1963, 4 acres were added when the Tennessee legislature provided the first public funds to accompany association funds. The Beaunit Corporation added 10 acres, including the bed of the Watauga River plus 10 feet of riverbank on both sides of the river and an island. A quitclaim deed, registered under Governor Clement on June 30, 1964, transferred Watauga River property to the State of Tennessee.

Playing a large part in the initiative's continued success were the research and writing of historian Mack Morris. His work was published in a ten-page brochure called *Watauga: The Dangerous Example*, which played a large part in securing Sycamore Shoals as a national historic landmark.

New funding was acquired when the City of Elizabethton and Carter County contributed $1,500 to the project; the state added funds of $3,500. A state engineering study and architectural master plan was then begun, based on the 1963 National Park Service plan.

The plan was endorsed by the Tennessee Conservation Department, and Sycamore Shoals was recommended to be the focal point for the state's bicentennial celebration in 1976. The Tennessee General Assembly, in 1971, appropriated $500,000 toward the plan's implementation plus appropriations added to purchase the John and Landon Carter Mansion property. A warranty deed purchased additional land at Sycamore Shoals and the Carter Mansion in June 1973.

With national-level support growing, on January 25, 1974, the National Park Service, U.S. Department of the Interior added Sycamore Shoals and the John and Landon Carter Mansion to the National Register of Historic Places. The Sycamore Shoals lands had earlier been placed on the National Register in 1966.

During the annual membership meeting of the Watauga Historical Association on November 19, 1973, the message they had been waiting for was announced by Senator Marshall Nave, who stated, "The Sycamore Shoals State Historical Park project has been approved by the State Building Commission and will be included in the budget of the State Conservation Department for 1974 to be submitted to the legislature." The consulting engineers retained for the project were the Wallace-Spoden firm of Kingsport, who planned to start construction work by early summer 1974.

An enormous amount of detailed research was conducted by Pollyanna Creekmore, primary source researcher, and Muriel Spoden, secondary source researcher, for the purpose of documenting Sycamore Shoals'

Left: Construction started on the new state park in the early summer of 1974. *Courtesy of Sycamore Shoals State Historic Park.*

Below: The Carter Mansion in the early 1970s when first purchased by the State of Tennessee. *Courtesy of Sycamore Shoals State Historic Park.*

history. Their research included books, documents, and letters of the late eighteenth-century Watauga settlers and longhunters, and the American Revolution. Additionally, articles published in journals and original paper documents such as land records, pension records, wills, and birth, marriage, and death records housed in libraries and, sometimes, personal collections, assisted their work.

The result was an excellent collection of sources and written history produced by Creekmore and Spoden, titled *Sycamore Shoals State Historic Park and Colonel John Carter Research*. It was edited and produced by H.T. Spoden and Associates for the Tennessee Historical Commission and the Tennessee Department of Conservation and completed in May 1974, including information about Sycamore Shoals State Park, the Colonel John Carter House, and the Watauga settlements. There are eight in-depth chapters plus an appendix on the Taylor family, the Carter family, and the Carter mansion; miscellaneous references; and an oral history by Judge Ben Allen.

After years of dedicated work that began prior to 1962, on Friday, July 2, 1976, Sycamore Shoals State Historic Area was dedicated during the nation's bicentennial celebration.

Today, the park is referred to as an historic park, and since 1976, the park staff, community, and historic reenactors have continued to honor and share the stories and lives of our eighteenth-century European ancestors and the Cherokee people. They work proudly and diligently toward upholding the park's mission of preservation and protection through education and interpretation of these remarkable stories.

Archaeological Studies and Building Fort Watauga

Fort Watauga was not a military fort; it is believed to have been located on the homeplace of Matthew Talbot, a miller and rancher. Talbot was also the first pastor of Sinking Creek Baptist Church. He and his wife, Mary, and their seven children came to Watauga from Virginia.

When the settlement received word of an imminent Cherokee attack, they had little time to prepare for the protection of their people. Thus, the Talbot family cabin and its outbuildings were graciously offered for protection. They served as the footprint of the fort, as each building was connected by constructing a log palisade wall.

The story of the archaeological work completed at the original fort site along with the building of a re-creation of Fort Watauga and the Cherokee attack on the fort in 1776 are discussed in detail in chapter 6.

Historic House Museums

The John and Landon Carter Mansion, Circa 1775–1780

The Carter mansion, a satellite of Sycamore Shoals, was purchased by the State of Tennessee in 1973. It is the oldest standing frame house in the state and was added to the National Register of Historic Places on January 25, 1974. After restoration of the house and archaeological work conducted on the grounds, the mansion officially opened to the public on June 17, 1981.

John Carter and his wife, Elizabeth Taylor, had three known children: Landon, John Jr., and Emmanuel. John Sr.'s first land claim was entered into the Watauga Purchase Book A on December 23, 1775, for a 640-acre tract on the south bank of the Watauga River, which included the mansion site. When John died of smallpox in 1780, Landon, his wife, Elizabeth MacLin, and their six children made the mansion their home. John Sr.'s other two sons had land adjoining their father's estate.

John Carter came to the Holson River from Virginia in the early 1770s and opened a trading post with William Parker with a plan to trade with the Cherokee. Carter and Parker were robbed by the Cherokee when they refused to travel to Cherokee villages to trade. Soon after, Carter and his family moved to Watauga, where he built a two-story frame house between 1775 and 1780. The oldest structure on the site, now gone, was constructed in the same manner as the mansion and may have served as Carter's first home and later a home for his enslaved people.

John's ancestry is a mystery of sorts as documents have not been found proving the identity of his parents. The documented people that were a part of his life in his earlier days suggest he was living in Virginia before coming

Possibly the first cabin built on the Carter Mansion property. *Courtesy of Sycamore Shoals State Historic Park.*

The Carter Mansion Celebration in 2015. *Courtesy of the author.*

John Carter served as entry taker for Washington County, North Carolina, surveying and entering acreage of land purchases for settlers. *Courtesy of Sycamore Shoals State Historic Park.*

This original portrait of Landon Carter, son of John, is on permanent display at Sycamore Shoals State Historic Park. *Courtesy of Sycamore Shoals State Historic Park.*

to the southwestern settlements. For many years, those who are interested in his ancestry, life, and acquaintances have found some support that suggests he could be descended from Robert King Carter of Virginia. This may never be proven, but the elaborate décor and overmantel paintings in the Carter Mansion do suggest he was raised among the finer things in life.

John quickly became a strong leader in the settlement. He served in the Watauga Association, chaired the Committee of Safety, was the entry taker who recorded land purchases, attained the military rank of colonel, and commanded Fort Watauga during the Cherokee attack of 1776. When Washington County was created, he served in the North Carolina legislature.

Landon also became a leader in the community, serving as a member of the North Carolina General Assembly, speaker of the senate and secretary of state for the State of Franklin, and a delegate to the Tennessee Constitutional Convention. Militarily, he earned the rank of brigadier general in the militia. The mansion stayed with the Carter family until 1877, when William S. Thomas purchased the property. Thomas's descendants lived there up until the late 1960s.

In December 1973, the year the property was purchased by the state from the Thomas family, preliminary archaeological testing was conducted under the direction of Sam D. Smith of the Division of Archaeology, Tennessee Department of Conservation. State archaeological site 40CR5 was complex as eighteenth- through twentieth-century occupation was evident. Prehistoric occupation that consisted of possibly several acres was also identified. The added north wing of the mansion, the Thomas addition, was removed, exposing an area with great archaeological potential on the river side of the house.

In the summer of 1977, Sam Smith planned a complete assessment of the archaeological remains on this 4.2-acre state-owned tract. Excavations yielding historic artifacts were limited to areas near the house. Interviews with the Thomas family and a 1949 TVA aerial photo confirmed the

Above: A section of the archaeological work conducted at Carter Mansion is pictured on the river side of the house. *Courtesy of Sycamore Shoals State Historic Park.*

Left, top: During restoration of the Carter Mansion in the 1970s, the siding was removed to examine the structure. In this image, you can see "joiners marks" III. The timber is marked with roman numerals to match up the beams correctly. *Courtesy of Sycamore Shoals State Historic Park.*

Left, bottom: In this image of the Carter Mansion, mud bricks, or nogging, are exposed between the outside and inside walls. They were used as insulation, to strengthen the timber frame structure, and for fire resistance, among other uses. *Courtesy of Sycamore Shoals State Historic Park.*

locations of the outbuildings. Smith learned that the Thomas family had uncovered evidence of Native occupation in 1927 when digging a flower pit. Henry Woodman, a field archaeologist working for the Smithsonian Institute, learned of this and spent April 1927 also digging on the site.

East Tennessee State University Professor Eileen G. Ernenwein and student Cayla Cannon conducted geophysical and additional archaeological studies during the 2016–17 school year. Tools used included ground-penetrating radar, magnetometry, and related equipment. Historic structures from the Carter era into the nineteenth century were detected along with prehistoric features. Excavations of prehistoric sites revealed fire pits, dumping piles, and artifacts. Dating of artifacts indicated Native people occupied the site from about AD 1500–1770; European settlement had begun there by 1770. These dates also correspond to similar Mississippian sites on the Watauga and Nolichucky Rivers.

The interior of the Carter home reflects the past lives of people who probably came from families of means. The front entrance opens into the Great Hall, with a parlor and Carter's office to the left. Upstairs is a master bedroom, a smaller bedroom, a landing, and a set of stairs to the attic. Every room has a fireplace except for the small upstairs bedroom. Color and design are present throughout the house: chair railing, denticular crown molding, fireplace mantels with decorative carvings, hand-carved panels, a main staircase, and an inset corner cabinet. The overmantel paintings in John Carter's office and the master bedroom are paintings applied directly to the wood, illustrating what may be images from an earlier home. During the restoration, Cynthia Kelsey Stowe of the Cumberland Art Conservation Center cleaned and restored the two overmantel paintings.

Pottery fragments found at the Carter Mansion also corresponded to pottery found at sites on the Nolichucky River and the Watauga River. *Courtesy of Sycamore Shoals State Historic Park.*

Historic paint finishes specialist Matthew J. Mosca conducted two separate studies of this home, documenting the earliest presence of pigments and decorative effects not previously studied. In 2018, a study was conducted on the first floor of surfaces that

Top: The overmantel painting in the master bedchamber depicts a scene that some historians believe could be from John Carter's past. *Courtesy of Frank Jarboe.*

Bottom: Restoration of the overmantel painting in the 1970s in Carter's office on the first floor. *Courtesy of Sycamore Shoals State Historic Park.*

had been overpainted in addition to surfaces that had not been overpainted. Small samples were taken in each room and studied using different types of microscopy; the goal was to identify the original pigments, decorative effects, and media used.

Many of the walls, floors, and ceilings have not been covered with wallpaper, modern paint, or anything that would damage the original interior finishes. This is a rarity: Most historic houses are redecorated when the ownership changes or when the property is passed to the next generation.

An important consideration is that pigments deteriorate over time and can appear different from their original color. For instance, an original finish in the Great Hall was a light greenish blue. Over time, it turned light brown as the Prussian blue faded and the oil medium browned. In 1978, when the house was restored, the process of discoloration was not well understood. If a wall appeared brown, it was repainted brown, when, in fact, its original finish—as in this case—may have been a light greenish blue. Another complication is that it appears that the woodwork was "touched up" in the past as needed so that modern, contemporary finishes do not match the original historic finishes.

A second finish in the hall was originally a brilliant green varnish, used over a light ground. "Crystals of verdigris" is a salt derived from a solution of copper in vinegar. When dissolved in a varnish, it can retain its green color for many years, but eventually it turns black. Also found was a splatter pattern from a twentieth-century finish on surfaces that emulates the appearance of granite stone. The hall mantel had original, never painted areas of the fine Prussian blue color found under a later trim molding.

The parlor's woodwork is exceptional and has not been overpainted except for the ceiling and fireplace mantel. The presence of early Prussian blue on the wall panels and in other locations is significant. This original finish remains exposed. Details of the painter's methods can also be seen in this room.

Carter's office walls were not painted for a number of years. The first finish was white lead with a continuous painted baseboard of lamp black.

On the first floor, the significant pigments identified as first finishes were white lead, massicot/yellow monoxide of lead, lamp black, brown ochres and umbers, and Prussian blue. The verdigris green pigment was added at a later date during the very extended exposure period of the first finish.

In 2020, Mosca returned to the mansion to study the second floor, which is of great importance due to its eighteenth-century authenticity. The second-floor landing and master bedchamber, remarkably, have all the original marbling finishes exposed. Additionally, the flat pine surfaces were painted to also simulate wood veneer and wood paneling. The fascia around the outside of the stairs is painted with a combination of white lead and Prussian blue.

The master bedchamber's decorative finishes are mostly exposed. Of interest is the pink and white marbled finish, one of the most important features of the mansion. *Courtesy of Sycamore Shoals State Historic Park.*

Significant finishes from the second floor were the same as the first floor with the addition of yellow ochres, red ochres, and vermillion. The two bedrooms on the second floor also retain their earliest finishes. The pink and white marbled finish in the West Bedchamber is particularly extraordinary and one of the most important features of the Carter mansion.

Based on these studies, our understanding of the Carter Mansion is enhanced with added research and data that support the importance of this home and reflect on the lives of those who lived there. Mosca stated, "Original finishes from the eighteenth century are extraordinarily rare and must be retained." In the case of the Carter Mansion, original paint layers are over 240 years old.

In the mid-2000s, the Carter Mansion was named in the will of David Davis, who left the site approximately twenty pieces of historic furniture from the late eighteenth century and earlier. His kindness truly brought the home to life. Several of these pieces were identified in the Will of Elizabeth Carter, wife of Landon Carter, though there is not evidence to indicate they came from the mansion.

The importance of the Carter family and the pride the community holds in its history are reflected in Carter County being named for Landon Carter and the city of Elizabethton for Landon's wife, Elizabeth. Today, that same feeling holds true.

When visiting the mansion today, you will find a visitors' center and museum along with an historic family cemetery on the site, which rests beside the Watauga River. House tours are conducted throughout the year along with seasonal programs.

Sabine Hill State Historic Site, Circa 1818

Approaching Elizabethton at its western entrance stands a beautiful Federal period frame home on a hill overlooking the Watauga River. It is now considered the finest standing example of wood-framed Federal architecture in the state of Tennessee.

Oral history has indicated that the house was constructed between 1816 and 1818 and possibly begun by Brigadier General Nathaniel Taylor. Taylor contracted malaria during the War of 1812 and died in February 1816 at his Sycamore Shoals plantation following his military service, so he would not have seen the house completed.

Sabine Hill State Historic Site was constructed circa 1818. It was purchased by the Tennessee Historical Commission and opened to the public in 2017. *Courtesy of Sycamore Shoals State Historic Park.*

Sabine Hill from the back with the detached kitchen, surrounded by a colorful pollinator garden. *Courtesy of the author.*

To assist in dating the house, dendroarchaeological studies were conducted by Henry Grissino-Mayer and students from the University of Tennessee in October 2013, which involved taking forty-two core samples from twenty-six beams and logs making up the primary house structure. Older logs supporting the first floor in the basement were hand-hewn, while others had intact bark. All samples were from the white oak group. Tree ring data was compared to an absolutely dated oak data set from the International Tree-Ring Data Bank. This data set consisted of thirteen oak chronologies from East Tennessee to western North Carolina and western Virginia. Their team returned in May 2014 to study the attic structure, which yielded some rafters with saw marks indicative of early nineteenth-century water-powered sash saws, most likely original to the structure.

The outcome of the study indicated that trees harvested to build Sabine Hill were cut in the early spring of 1818, ending in the spring of 1819. In this case, the data suggests that the first trees were cut about two years after Nathaniel's death and that the house would have been built by his widow, Mary, who lived in the house and ran the family's farm until her death in 1853.

The Archaeological Research Lab from the University of Tennessee, working under Dr. Elizabeth J. Kellar, studied the grounds surrounding the house using ground-penetrating radar and excavated near the house. The study yielded little information related to the occupation period of the house and before, as the grounds had been turned for agricultural use for many years. Some early projectile points in addition to pottery were discovered.

Nathaniel's father, Andrew, was the first Taylor in Watauga, arriving in 1778 when Nathaniel was seven years old. His land and home bordered today's Sabine Hill property. Joseph Tipton Sr. sold Nathaniel 381 acres in 1809, which now includes the Sabine site. Over time, the family acquired 3,000 acres of land, which they fondly named Happy Valley. Nathaniel married Mary Patton of Rockbridge County, Virginia, and had eight children. Several of their children and grandchildren become very successful in adulthood. Brothers Alf Alexander Taylor and Bob Love Taylor, their great-grandsons, are known for their 1886 political campaign, the War of the Roses, running against each other for the governor's seat in Tennessee. Both men served terms in the governorship.

Nathaniel, a strong leader, served in the military, community, and business. Some of his accomplishments include being appointed justice of the peace for Washington County-Southwest Territory, becoming the first sheriff of Carter County, being commissioned to establish county boundaries, and serving as trustee to the town's leading school, the Duffield Academy. He also served in both houses of the Tennessee legislature.

Taylor was promoted to the rank of brigadier general in 1804, commanding a regiment of Tennessee troops. During the War of 1812, he and the East Tennessee Militia served under General Andrew Jackson in Mobile, Alabama. Ultimately, Nathaniel Taylor became one of the wealthiest men in Carter County, engaging in many business ventures including the manufacture of bar iron, flour, and gunpowder.

Seeding a newly turned field with pollinator species in early nineteenth-century attire on the west side of the Sabine Hill house. *Courtesy of Sycamore Shoals State Historic Park.*

The home of the brigadier general was placed on the National Register of Historic Places on January 25, 1974. When the Historic American Buildings Survey, the nation's first federal preservation program, began in 1933, Sabine Hill was one of four buildings documented in Carter County. Respected historian and author, Judge Samuel Cole Williams, was referenced in the HABS report as saying, "This [is] one of the most outstanding landmarks in Tennessee—Taylor employed a Philadelphia architect who may have been influenced by Williamsburg, Virginia architecture."

The interior boasts elaborate architecture and fine interior finishes, with beautiful carved mantles in most rooms. Colorful historic paint finishes and styles are seen throughout. Historic paint finishes specialist Matthew J. Mosca conducted in-depth studies in 2013 and 2014, finding much of the original fabric of the home still intact. Marbling techniques on wood were discovered on the stair risers and below chair rails, in addition to stippled marbling in the east parlor. Three predominant pigments used in the house were lead white, rich Prussian blue, and red mahogany graining. Many areas of the house retain original fireplace mantles, doors, stairs, stair rails, floors, and walls.

Deeds indicate that after Mary Taylor's death in 1853, the property remained in the possession of her heirs until 1949, primarily operated by

Left: After exposing examples of original marbling on portions of the stair risers, decorative painter Cass Holly re-created the original look in color and pattern. *Courtesy of Sycamore Shoals State Historic Park.*

Below: Decorate finishes can be seen in the West Parlor on the mantel, wood panels, and wallpaper. All decorative work during the restoration was based on evidence and studies determining what was originally there. *Courtesy of Sycamore Shoals State Historic Park.*

Left: Matthew Mosca, historic paint specialist, is seen collecting small samples below the modern paint to determine colors and finishes used. *Courtesy of Sycamore Shoals State Historic Park.*

Below: The best surviving example of the original Prussian blue finish was found in the door frame of the master bedchamber. *Courtesy of Sycamore Shoals State Historic Park.*

Opposite: When the Reynold's family purchased the property in the late 1940s, the house had been vacant for quite some time. This image was taken in 1949. *Courtesy of Sycamore Shoals State Historic Park.*

tenant farmers. James L. Reynolds purchased the old home in 1949, hoping to restore it to its original splendor. He and the subsequent property owner worked on the house as time and money permitted, but the enormity of the project made complete restoration difficult.

Time and the elements took a toll on the structure. Taylor descendants such as Dr. B. Harrison Taylor and others continually worked behind the scenes trying to save the home. It took a crisis to bring this need to the forefront. In 2007, the house was about to be purchased by a contractor, who intended to demolish it and build forty-six condominiums. As a result, Sabine Hill was placed on the Tennessee Preservation Trust's list of the Top Ten Endangered Historic Treasures.

Jerry Wooten, working with the Tennessee Historical Commission, met with Helen Wilson, chairwoman of the Elizabethton Historic Zoning Commission, and former Elizabethton Mayor Sam LaPorte. With just a week to spare, Wilson and Mayor LaPorte bought the property and sold it in 2008 to the State of Tennessee for future restoration.

As time passed, the home's foundation became critically in need of repair. Searching for grants had not brought forth any funding, so when the Coca-Cola Bottling Company's 2011 America's Favorite Parks competition came to light, it seemed worthy of a try. The top three parks with the highest vote totals would win funding.

Sycamore Shoals State Historic Park started in 3,656th place when the competition was discovered, but the park staff and the community came together for a cause and generated a high number of votes. Amazingly, Sycamore Shoals ended the competition in fourth place! Though no money was won, in the end, the outcome was even better. The people had spoken, and the next fiscal year, Governor Bill Haslam's budget included $1.1 million in Tennessee Historical Commission funding for the restoration of Sabine Hill State Historic Site in Elizabethton.

Sabine Hill State Historic Site, dedicated in 2017, is now operated in partnership between the Tennessee Historic Commission and Sycamore Shoals State Historic Park. Park interpreters offer guided tours of the Taylor home throughout the year in addition to special events. On the grounds, you can enjoy the view of the Watauga River, browse interpretive signage along the walkway, and take in a native plant garden covering close to an acre. Future plans include the construction of a new visitors' center at this site.

Through the dedication of the community and Taylor descendants coupled with the support of the Tennessee Historic Commission and Tennessee State Parks, Sabine Hill is once again alive with stories, history, and experiences that will take us back to the earliest days of Nathaniel and Mary Taylor and their family.

Preserving History Through Interpretation and Inspiration

Park interpretive staff and rangers offer a myriad of interpretive programs, special events, and historic house tours at scheduled times throughout the year. Many special events include the assistance of historic reenactors who are members of the Washington County Regiment of the North Carolina militia, individuals and families with a love for history and a desire to share it

Eighteenth-century reenactors volunteering at Sycamore Shoals are passionate about the history and sharing it with park visitors. *Courtesy of Sycamore Shoals State Historic Park.*

Above, left: Waiting patiently. *Courtesy of Sycamore Shoals State Historic Park.*

Above, right: Revolutionary War period games for the young and their families. *Courtesy of Sycamore Shoals State Historic Park.*

Left: Processing flax to make linen thread. *Courtesy of Sycamore Shoals State Historic Park.*

with others. This volunteer organization was preceded by the support of the Company of Overmountain Men, organized under the leadership of Grant Hardin. In addition to park-sponsored organizations, the community has embraced its past since long before the creation of the state park.

Regional Celebrations and Events

The citizens of Elizabethton have not forgotten the significant contributions of their ancestors, and their pride in past accomplishments is seen in many ways. Recently, an old program surfaced from September 25, 1900, when the County Court of Carter County ordered a celebration of the "120th anniversary of the assembling of the heroes of Kings Mountain at Sycamore Shoals." The highlight of the event was the erection of a monument in commemoration of the event. Food, music, and speakers brought honor to the event. Keynote speaker the Honorable Samuel Arnell represented the Washington County Historical Society.

The first known documented historical drama in Elizabethton, Tennessee, occurred on October 7, 1922, when the community presented Watauga Association Day, featuring an outdoor drama named *The Pageant of Freedom*. It was presented at Sycamore Shoals to honor the 150th anniversary of the Watauga Association and was directed by Oliver Taylor with a large cast of nearly two hundred performers portraying historical characters.

Divided into five episodes, the drama covered the important history of Sycamore Shoals, ending with a focus on 1917 and the veterans and war

The first outdoor drama at Sycamore Shoals, *The Transylvania Purchase*, was performed in October 1975. *Courtesy of Sycamore Shoals State Historic Park.*

The actors and actresses presenting *The Wataugans* were all volunteers whose purpose was to keep the history of Sycamore Shoals alive from generation to generation. *Courtesy of Sycamore Shoals State Historic Park.*

workers of the recently ended World War I. Considering the timing of this event, it most likely was very meaningful to those involved and in attendance.

The first drama at the state park was a one-act play written by Ronnie Day on the Transylvania purchase and performed in October 1975 at Sycamore Shoals. *The Wataugans*, a three-act outdoor drama also written by Ronnie Day, debuted for one night at Sycamore Shoals in 1979 and 1980. During the third season of *The Wataugans*, a special presentation took place on September 25, 1981, the evening of the muster of the Overmountain Men. From its beginning, the drama has continued annually. With attendance increasing, the drama ran for six nights in 1982 for over four thousand guests. In 2001, *The Wataugans* was designated the Official Outdoor Drama of the State of Tennessee. It was presented by the Watauga Historical Association and Sycamore Shoals State Historic Area each year in July through 2006.

Friends of Sycamore Shoals

Friends of Sycamore Shoals became a nonprofit corporation in February 2007 and became the volunteer support group for the state park. Since its inception, it has engaged in fundraising, volunteerism, and memberships along with its support of interpretive programming, projects both large and small, and public outreach.

The Friends group continued the legacy begun with the outdoor drama *The Wataugans* in 1979 under a new name and a new script, introducing *Liberty!: The Saga of Sycamore Shoals* in July 2007. On July 20, 2009, *Liberty!* was recognized as the Official Outdoor Drama of the State of Tennessee, and it is now presented annually during the month of June. In 2024, *Liberty!* opened in a completely new amphitheater, funded by the Friends group, which has also acquired state-of-the-art sound and lighting for the show.

The Washington County Regiment of North Carolina Militia, mentioned earlier, is also supported by the Friends group, as is the Sabine Hill Social Society, which maintains a goal of sharing the dance, stories, lifeways, and

The muster of the Overmountain Men was a must in both *Wataugans* and *Liberty!* outdoor dramas. *Courtesy of Sycamore Shoals State Historic Park.*

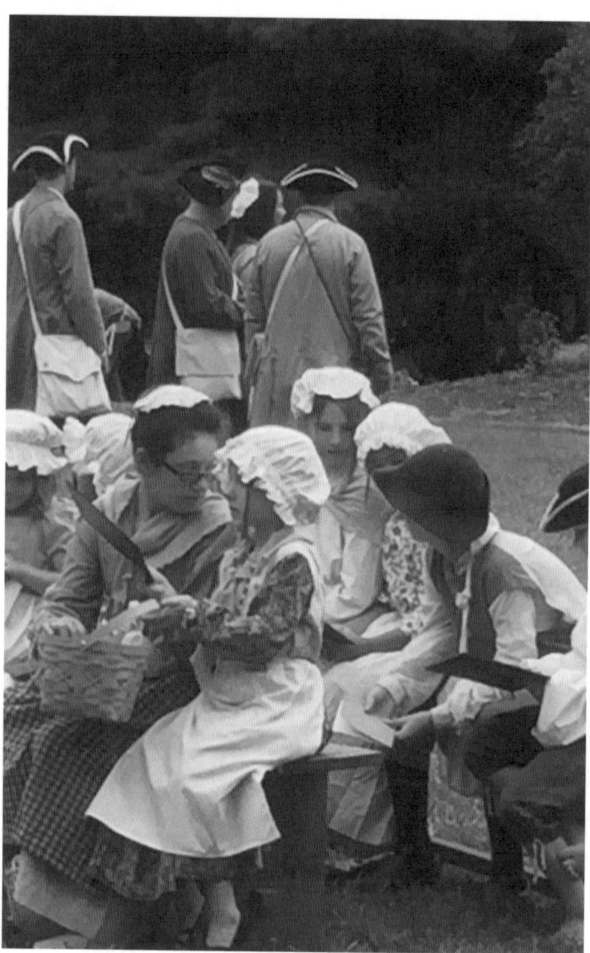

The outdoor drama *Liberty! The Saga of Sycamore Shoals* began in 2007 at the state park. This scene portrays a school scene on the frontier. *Courtesy of Sycamore Shoals State Historic Park.*

history of the Jeffersonian era, which spans the presidencies of Thomas Jefferson and James Madison. After the War of 1812, this era continued and was also referred to as the Era of Good Feelings.

Overmountain Victory Trail Association (OVTA)

The bicentennial of the American Revolution, April 1, 1975, included events that took place nationwide to honor the memory of this war. Celebrations continued through July 4, 1976, the two hundredth year since the Declaration of Independence was signed.

Members of the Overmountain Victory Trail Association and friends cross the Watauga River at Sycamore Shoals on September 25 each year to walk in the footsteps of their Patriot and Loyalist ancestors, completing their journey at Kings Mountain, South Carolina. Photo: 1980s. *Courtesy of Sycamore Shoals State Historic Park.*

During the annual river crossing on September 25, the reenactors pause to fire a volley in memory of their ancestors. *Courtesy of the author.*

Citizens and descendants of Patriots and Loyalists came together on September 25, 1975, to follow the route of the Overmountain Men to Kings Mountain in 1780. The first people who marched in 1975 became the founders of the Overmountain Victory Trail Association, chartered in 1979, which exists today. Its earliest goal was to encourage public support for the creation of a National Historic Trail designation. Success came in September 1980 with the official designation of the Overmountain Victory National Historic Trail, signed into law by President Jimmy Carter. On October 7, 1980, the two hundredth anniversary march took place, traveling from Abingdon, Virginia, to the muster grounds of Sycamore Shoals and through North Carolina, ending at Kings Mountain National Military Park in Blacksburg, South Carolina.

To this day, the dedication of the OVTA continues with the annual remembrance march, reenacted by interpreters, citizens, and descendants of the 1780 Overmountain Men. The Kings Mountain Chapter of the Company of Overmountain Men is active in organizing the annual event. Beginning each year on September 23 in Abingdon, Virginia, they cross the Watauga River at the Sycamore Shoals muster grounds on September 25. Throughout their journey, they dedicate their time to providing educational programs to school groups and the public. A commemorative motor route and associated brochure can be accessed through the National Park Service.

Dedication of the Interpretive Museum

When the park was officially opened in 1976, it included a visitors' center, nearly one-third of which was meant to be an interpretive museum. Over time, part of the space was used for exhibits, and the remainder of the large room was used for programs and events.

After 2010, funding came forth to build a quality interpretive museum to share the Sycamore Shoals story. This long-awaited dream soon came to fruition. Troy McCormick of Natural Concepts was contracted as the designer, and Essyx Design and Fabrication created the exhibits.

The museum was dedicated on June 26, 2013, to a large group who had long anticipated this moment. The Watauga Valley Fife and Drum performed, Washington County Militia interpreters interacted with park guests, and Tennessee State Parks Chief Ranger Shane Petty welcomed guests with his horse, Dodge Hemi, as they approached the visitors' center.

The Washington County Regiment of North Carolina militia is in formation for the dedication of the new Interpretive Museum at Sycamore Shoals. *Courtesy of Sycamore Shoals State Historic Park.*

Production of the new museum's interpretive film couldn't go forward without historic reenactors to fill the many roles of the story. *Courtesy of Sycamore Shoals State Historic Park.*

Tennessee State Governor Bill Haslam and Department of Environment and Conservation Commissioner Bob Martineau were both in attendance along with community and state park leaders. Beautiful murals were created from the original paintings of artist Richard Luce, commissioned for this project; realistic mannequins in period clothing were dressed in eighteenth-century attire, dyed with native plant colors and handsewn by Susie and Steve Ricker; and a re-creation of Fort Watauga was installed, alongside many other individuals' contributions and exhibits. A highlight was the creation of a small theater and a new movie, *Sycamore Shoals: Story of the American Spirit*, which was presented entirely by historic reenactors.

Since the museum's opening in 2013, exhibits have been added, and they now continue into the entrance lobby of the park. The large glass window on the back of the building creates an overlook that frames the recreation of Fort Watauga. A visit to the park visitors' center is, without a doubt, an immersive historic experience.

When visiting Sycamore Shoals State Historic Park in Elizabethton, Tennessee, you will find yourself walking in the footsteps of people of many cultures who have passed through over time. The eighteenth-century Patriots, dedicated to the concept of liberty and independence from Great Britain, along with the Cherokee who first inhabited these lands, came long before us. Whether you are touring on your own or attending a special event, ranger program, reenactment, or historic house tour, you are sure to be inspired and humbled by the stories you will hear.

Inside of the park's visitors' center, you will find a gift shop with a myriad of items, including books that are related to the park's themes; the interpretive museum that brings stories to life; a large room for meetings and events at one end of the building; and a picnic area beside the building. Between the visitors' center and Watauga River is a re-creation of historic Fort Watauga, an outdoor amphitheater, a walking trail along the Watauga River, a butterfly garden near the walking trail, and picnic shelters.

The two historic house museums, the Carter Mansion and Sabine Hill State Historic Site, are located off-site and are within a short drive of the state historic park. Sabine Hill is managed by the Tennessee Historic Commission and operated in partnership with Sycamore Shoals State Historic Park.

In nearby Johnson City, a ten-mile drive from Sycamore Shoals will take you to Tipton Haynes State Historic Site, where the Battle of the State of Franklin took place. You can also visit Rocky Mount State Historic Site in Piney Flats, the capital of the Southwest Territory and historic Jonesborough, Tennessee's oldest town, both just fourteen miles from Sycamore Shoals.

NOTES

Chapter 1

1. Roos, "Early Humans."
2. Willerslev et al., "Genetic Records," 791–95; Slon et al., "Neandertal and Denisovan DNA," 605–08.
3. Davis and Madsen, "Coastal Migration Theory," 1–22.
4. Pigati et al., "Footprints at White Sands," 73–75.
5. Ramsey, *Annals of Tennessee*, 32.
6. Williams, *Dawn of Tennessee Valley*, 4–8.
7. Williams, *Dawn of Tennessee Valley*, 9.
8. Williams, *Dawn of Tennessee Valley*, 13–14.
9. Williams, *Dawn of Tennessee Valley*, 14–17.
10. Williams, *Dawn of Tennessee Valley*, 56–57.
11. Williams, *Early Travels*, 19–23, 24–28.
12. Ramsey, *Annals of Tennessee*, 43.

Chapter 2

13. King, *Cherokee Indian Nation*, ix.
14. Western Carolina University, "Research Guides."
15. Sampeck et al., "Geographic Information System Modeling," 46–66.
16. Sampeck et al., "Geographic Information System Modeling," 50–63.
17. Shreve et al., "Contact, Colonialism," 152–55.

18. Calloway, *America's First Western Frontier*, 35–37.
19. Museum of the Cherokee People; Eastern Band of Cherokee Indians.
20. Williams, *Tennessee During the Revolutionary War*, 31, 48; Woodward, *Cherokees*, 96–97.
21. Stoneberg, "1882 Bison Population Collapse," 106–14

Chapter 3

22. Hyder, *Watauga Old Fields*, 253–55.
23. Williams, *Dawn of Tennessee Valley*, 344.
24. Williams, *Dawn of Tennessee Valley*, 340–41.
25. Williams, *Dawn of Tennessee Valley*, 341–42.
26. Williams, *Dawn of Tennessee Valley*, 341.
27. Williams, *Dawn of Tennessee Valley*, 348.
28. Williams, *Dawn of Tennessee Valley*, 348.
29. Herndon, *William Tatham*, 348–51.
30. Irwin, *Voice in the Wilderness*, 238–53.

Chapter 4

31. Dixon, *Wataugans*, 12.
32. Garrett and Goodpasture, *History of Tennessee*, 54–56.
33. Williams, *Dawn of Tennessee Valley*, 367.
34. Dixon, *Wataugans*, 14.
35. Fisk, "Summary Notice," 21.
36. Dixon, *Wataugans*, 14.
37. Williams, *Dawn of Tennessee Valley*, 372–77.
38. Williams, *Tennessee During the Revolutionary War*, 75–80.
39. Garrett and Goodpasture, *History of Tennessee*, 56–57.
40. Dixon, *Wataugans*, 10.
41. Dixon, *Wataugans*, 10.

Chapter 5

42. Moore, *Frontier Mind*; Bakeless, *Daniel Boone*, 83.
43. Henderson, *Conquest of the Old Southwest*, 200–03; Bakeless, *Daniel Boone*, 82–83.

44. Henderson, *Conquest of the Old Southwest*, 108, 149–50, 200–03.
45. Henderson, *Conquest of the Old Southwest*, 217–20.
46. Fries, *Moravians in North Carolina*, 835–36; Williams, *Dawn of Tennessee Valley*, 403.
47. Fries, *Moravians in North Carolina*, 835–36.
48. Kincaid, *Wilderness Road*, 93–95.
49. Williams, *Dawn of Tennessee Valley*, 405.
50. Bakeless, *Daniel Boone*, 84–86.
51. Creekmore and Spoden, "Historical Research," 263; Dixon, *Wataugans*, 29.
52. Creekmore and Spoden, "Historical Research," 263.
53. Williams, *Dawn of Tennessee Valley*, 412–13; Dixon, *Wataugans*, 30.
54. Williams, *Dawn of Tennessee Valley*, 411.
55. Williams, *Dawn of Tennessee Valley*, 430–37.
56. Bakeless, *Daniel Boone*, 83–84.
57. Washington, *Writings of George Washington*, 279.

Chapter 6

58. Dixon, *Wataugans*, 39; Hamer, *Correspondence*, 451.
59. Dixon, *Wataugans*, 44.
60. Dixon, *Wataugans*, 42–43.
61. Hamer, *Correspondence*, 69.
62. Hamer, *Correspondence*, 70.
63. Creekmore and Spoden, "Historical Research," 438.
64. NC Secretary of State, *Colonial Records*, 712–13.
65. Ramsey, *Annals of Tennessee*, 150–51.
66. Williams, *Dawn of Tennessee Valley*, 46–47.
67. Draper, *Kings Mountain*, 420.
68. Alderman, *Overmountain Men*, 45–48.
69. Williams, *William Tatham*, 20.
70. Draper, *Kings Mountain*, 420.
71. Goodspeed, *History of Tennessee*, 970.
72. Inman, "Dark and Bloody Ground," 258–75.
73. Williams, *Tennessee During the Revolutionary War*, 75–79, 83–84.

Chapter 7

74. Adams, *Rights of Colonists*, 417–28.

75. Powell, "Spark of Revolution."
76. Williams, *Dawn of Tennessee Valley*, 391–97.
77. Dixon, *Wataugans*, 36.
78. Williams, *Tennessee During the Revolutionary War*, 32–34.
79. Williams, *Tennessee During the Revolutionary War*, 49.
80. Williams, *Tennessee During the Revolutionary War*, 49.
81. Williams *Tennessee During the Revolutionary War*, 54
82. Williams, *Tennessee During the Revolutionary War*, 69–71.
83. Woodward, *Cherokees*, 116.

Chapter 8

84. Williams, *Tennessee During the Revolutionary War*, 130.
85. Ramsey, *Annals of Tennessee*, 215.
86. Williams, *Tennessee During the Revolutionary War*, 131.
87. Draper, *Kings Mountain*, 107.
88. Draper, *Kings Mountain*, 109.
89. Williams, *Tennessee During the Revolutionary War*, 135–16; Draper, *Kings Mountain*, 118.
90. Williams, *Tennessee During the Revolutionary War*, 135.
91. Draper, *Kings Mountain*, 149.
92. Williams, *Tennessee During the Revolutionary War*, 141; Draper, *Kings Mountain*, 562.
93. Draper, *Kings Mountain*, 170.
94. Draper, *Kings Mountain*, 170.
95. Ramsey, *Annals of Tennessee*, 174.
96. Draper, *Kings Mountain*, 175.
97. Williams, *Tennessee During the Revolutionary War*, 144–45.
98. Ramsey, *Annals of Tennessee*, 229.
99. Williams, *Tennessee During the Revolutionary War*, 146.
100. Draper, *Kings Mountain*, 180–81.
101. Draper, *Kings Mountain*, 203–04.
102. Williams, *Tennessee During the Revolutionary War*, 151.
103. Williams, *Tennessee During the Revolutionary War*, 155.
104. Williams, *Tennessee During the Revolutionary War*, 156.
105. Williams, *Tennessee During the Revolutionary War*, 157.
106. Williams, *Tennessee During the Revolutionary War*, 155.
107. Williams, *Tennessee During the Revolutionary War*, 159.
108. Draper, *Kings Mountain*, 588.

109. McGill, "Joseph Greer," 40–42, 204–07.
110. Draper, *Kings Mountain*, 342–43.
111. Williams, *Tennessee During the Revolutionary War*, 159–61.
112. Draper, *Kings Mountain*, 344–45.
113. Draper, *Kings Mountain*, 345–46.
114. Williams, *Tennessee During the Revolutionary War*, 183–84.
115. Williams, *Tennessee During the Revolutionary War*, 196–98.
116. Williams, *Tennessee During the Revolutionary War*, 217–19.
117. Williams, *Tennessee During the Revolutionary War*, 219–23.
118. Williams, *Tennessee During the Revolutionary War*, 223.
119. Haywood, *Civil and Political History*, 83–88, 118.

Chapter 9

120. Williams, *Lost State of Franklin*, 339.
121. Dixon, *Wataugans*, 65.
122. Ramsey, *Annals of Tennessee*, 337–38, 356–57.
123. Williams, *Lost State of Franklin*, 199.
124. Dixon, *Wataugans*, 66; Williams, *Lost State of Franklin*, 199, 426–29.
125. Fink, *State of Franklin*, 195–213; Dixon, *Wataugans*, 66.
126. Williams, *Lost State of Franklin*, 232–33.
127. Williams, *Lost State of Franklin*, 230.
128. Durham, *Before Tennessee*, 31–38.
129. Williams, *Lost State of Franklin*, 253.
130. Durham, *Before Tennessee*, 39.
131. Haywood, *State of Tennessee*. 273–74.
132. Haywood, *State of Tennessee*. 314–15.
133. Durham, *Before Tennessee*, 165, 172; Downes, "Indian Affairs," 240–68, 259.
134. Durham, *Before Tennessee*, 187–89.
135. Moore and Foster, *Tennessee*.
136. Williams, *Lost State of Franklin*, 254.

BIBLIOGRAPHY

Adams, Samuel. "The Rights of the Colonists: The Report of the Committee of Correspondence to the Boston Town Meeting, Nov. 20, 1772." https://history.hanover.edu/texts/adamss.html.

Alderman, Pat. *The Overmountain Men*. Overmountain Press, 1970.

Allen, Ben, and Dennis T Lawson. "The Wataugans and the 'Dangerous Example.'" *Tennessee Historical Quarterly* 26, no. 2 (1967): 137–47. https://www.jstor.org/stable/42622934.

Allison, John. *Dropped Stitches in Tennessee History*. Originally published 1897. Reprint, Overmountain Press, 1971.

Alvord, Clarence W. "Virginia and the West." *Mississippi Valley Historical Review* 3, no. 1 (June 1916): 19–38. https://www.jstor.org/stable/1887086.

Arthur, John Preston. *A History of Watauga County, North Carolina*. Overmountain Press, 1996.

———. *Western North Carolina: A History (From 1730 to 1913)*. Overmountain Press, 1996.

Bakeless, John. *Daniel Boone*. Originally published 1939. Reprint, Stackpole Books, 1965.

Bancroft, George. *History of the United States of America*. Originally published 1834. Reprint, Legare Street Press, 2023.

Barksdale, Kevin T. "Violence, Statecraft, and Statehood in the Early Republic: The State of Franklin, 1784–1788." In *Blood in the Hills: A History of Violence in Appalachia*, edited by Bruce E. Stewart. University Press of Kentucky, 2011.

Beck, Robin A. "From Joara to Chiaha: Spanish Exploration of the Appalachian Summit Area, 1540–1568." *Southeastern Archaeology* 16 (1997): 162–69.

Beck, Robin A., David G. Moore, and Christopher B. Rodning. "Identifying Fort San Juan: A Sixteenth-Century Spanish Occupation at the Berry Site, North Carolina." *Southeastern Archaeology* 25 (2006): 65–77.

Calhoun, William Gunn. *Samuel Doak, 1749–1830: His Life, His Children, Washington College*. Pioneer Printers, 1966.

Calloway, Brenda C. *America's First Western Frontier, East Tennessee: A Story of the Early Settlers and Indians of East Tennessee*. Overmountain Press, 1989.

Carter, Clarence Edward, ed. *The Territory South of the River Ohio, 1790–1796*. Vol. 4 of *The Territorial Papers of the United States*. U.S. Government Printing Office, 1936. Available via HathiTrust, https://www.hathitrust.org.

Cherokee Nation. "The History of the Cherokee Nation." June 4, 2019. https://www.cherokee.org.

Corkran, David H. *The Cherokee Frontier*. University of Oklahoma Press, 2016.

Creekmore, Pollyanna, and Muriel C. Spoden. "Historical Research: Sycamore Shoals State Park and Colonel John Carter House." Tennessee Historical Commission, Department of Conservation, and H.T. Spoden, May 1974.

Davis, Loren G., and David B. Madsen. "The Coastal Migration Theory: Formulation and Testable Hypotheses." *Quaternary Science Reviews* 249 (December 1, 2020): 106605. https://repository.library.noaa.gov/view/noaa/57365.

Decorse, Elizabeth Kellar, and Creswell, Bradley A. "Archaeological Testing at the Sabine Hill State Historic Site, Elizabethton, Carter County, Tennessee." University of Tennessee, June 2013.

Dicken, Roy S., Jr. *The Cherokee Indian Nation*. University of Tennessee Press, 1979.

Dickinson, Calvin. "Frontier Splendor: The Carter Mansion at Sycamore Shoals." *Tennessee Historical Quarterly* 41, no. 4 (1982): 317–25. https://www.jstor.org/stable/42626316.

Dickinson, W. Calvin, and Larry H. Whiteaker. "Pioneers in the Wilderness: Sycamore Shoals and the Settlement of Tennessee." Tennessee Department of Conservation, 1981.

Dixon, Max. *The Wataugans*. Originally published 1976. Reprint, Overmountain Press, 1989.

Downes, Randolph C. "Indian Affairs in the Southwest Territory, 1790–1796." *Tennessee Historical Magazine* 2nd ser., vol. 3, no. 4 (January 1937): 240–68. https://www.jstor.org/stable/42638127.

Draper, Lyman Copeland. "About the Draper Manuscript Collection." Wisconsin Historical Society, April 23, 2014. https://www.wisconsinhistory.org.

———. "Draper Manuscripts: Kentucky Papers, 1768–1892." Wisconsin Historical Society Digital Library. https://digicoll.library.wisc.edu.

———. "Kings Mountain and Its Heroes." Originally published 1881. Reprint, Overmountain Press, 1996.

———. "Kings Mountain Papers. Draper Manuscripts." Historical Society of Wisconsin, n.d.

Duncan, Barbara R, Brett H. Riggs, Museum of the Cherokee Indian, and Blue Ridge Heritage Initiative. *Cherokee Heritage Trails Guidebook*. Published in association with the Museum of the Cherokee Indian by the University of North Carolina Press, 2003.

Dunkerly, Robert M. *The Battle of Kings Mountain*. Arcadia Publishing, 2007.

———. *An Explorer's Guide to America's Revolutionary War: 250th Anniversary*. Blue and Gray Education Society, 2022.

Durham, Walter T. *Before Tennessee*. Originally published 1990. Reprint, Rocky Mount Historical Association, 2003.

Eastern Band of Cherokee Indians. https://visitcherokeenc.com.

Fink, Paul M. "Some Phases of the History of the State of Franklin." *Tennessee Historical Quarterly* 16, no. 3 (1957): 195–213. https://www.jstor.org/stable/43746574.

Fisk, Moses. "A Summary Notice of the First Settlements Made by the White People Within the Limits Which Bound the State of Tennessee." *Tennessee Historical Magazine* 2 (1897): 21.

Fleming, Thomas. *Liberty! The American Revolution*. Viking Adult, 1997.

Fleming, Thomas J. *The Intimate Lives of the Founding Fathers*. Smithsonian Books, 2010.

Foreman, Grant. *Sequoyah*. University of Oklahoma Press, 1977.

Foster, Dave. *Franklin the Stillborn State*. Overmountain Press, 2000.

Fries, Adelaide L. *Records of the Moravians in North Carolina*. Vol. 2. Edwards and Broughton Printing, 1922. Available via Moravian Archives, https://moravianarchives.org.

Garrett, William Robertson, and Albert Virgil Goodpasture. *History of Tennessee, Its People and Its Institutions*. Brandon Company, 1900. Available via Library of Congress, https://www.loc.gov.

Goodspeed Publishing Company. *Goodspeed's History of Tennessee*. N.d.

Grissino-Mayer, Henri D., Elizabeth A. Schneider, Maegen L. Rochner, Lauren A. Stachowiak, and Meagan E. Dennison. "Tree-Ring Dating of Timbers from Sabine Hill, Home of General Nathaniel Taylor, Elizabethton, Tennessee, USA." *Dendrochronologia* 43 (April 2017): 33–40. https://doi.org/10.1016/j.dendro.2016.09.001.

Halligan, Jessi J., Michael R. Waters, Angelina Perrotti, et al. "Pre-Clovis Occupation 14,550 Years Ago at the Page-Ladson Site, Florida, and the Peopling of the Americas." *Science Advances* 2, no. 5 (May 1, 2016): e1600375. https://www.science.org.

Hamer, Philip M. "Correspondence of Henry Stuart and Alexander Cameron with the Wataugans." *Mississippi Valley Historical Review* 17, no. 3 (December 1930): 451. https://www.jstor.org/stable/i305487.

Hamer, Philip M. Review of *Tennessee During the Revolutionary War* by Samuel Cole Williams. *Journal of Southern History* 11, no. 1 (February 1945): 107. https://www.jstor.org/stable/i312148.

Hamer, Philip M. *Tennessee: A History 1673–1932*. Vol. 1. American Historical Society, 1933.

Hamilton, J.G. de Roulhac. "Kings Mountain Letters of Col. Isaac Shelby." *Journal of Southern History* 4, no. 3 (August 1938): 367–77. https://doi.org/10.2307/2191295.

Harkness, David J. *Colonial Heroines of Tennessee, Kentucky and Virginia*. University of Tennessee Press, 1974.

Haywood, John. *The Civil and Political History of the State of Tennessee from Its Earliest Settlement up to the Year 1796*. Publishing House of the Methodist Episcopal Church, South, 1891.

Henderson, Archibald. *The Conquest of the Old Southwest*. Originally published 1920. Reprint, Library of Alexandria, 1920.

Herndon, G. Melvin. *William Tatham and the Culture of Tobacco*. University of Miami Press, 1969.

Hudson, Charles M. *The Southeastern Indians*. University of Tennessee Press, 1994.

Hudson, Charles M., and Paul E. Hoffman. *The Juan Pardo Expeditions: Explorations of the Carolinas and Tennessee, 1566–1568*. University of Alabama Press, 2005.

Huhta, James. "Tennessee and the American Revolutionary Bicentennial." *Tennessee Historical Quarterly* 31 (1976): 314.

Hyder, N.E. "Watauga Old Fields." *American Historical Magazine* 8, no. 3 (July 1903): 253–55.

Inman, Natalie. "'A Dark and Bloody Ground': American Indian Responses to Expansion During the American Revolution." *Tennessee Historical Quarterly* 70, no. 4 (November 2011): 258–75. https://www.jstor.org/stable/42628217.

Irwin, Ned L. "Voice in the Wilderness: John Haywood and the Preservation of Early Tennessee History." *Tennessee Historical Quarterly* 58, no. 3 (1999): 238–53. http://www.jstor.org/stable/42628484.

Jones, Randell. *A Guide to the Overmountain Victory National Historic Trail*. Daniel Boone Footsteps, 2011.

Keesee, Troy Ronald. *The Wataugah Land Purchases*. Originally published 1997. Reprint, Wisdom Way Publishing, 2007.

Kennedy, Roger G. *Architecture, Men, Women and Money in America, 1600–1860*. Random House, 1985.

Kilgore, Jenny L. "The Carter Mansion Revisited." Master's thesis, East Tennessee State University, 2007. https://www.mobt3ath.com/uplode/book/book-122021.pdf.

Kincaid, Robert Lee. *The Wilderness Road*. 3rd ed. 1947. Lincoln Memorial University Press, 1955.

King, Duane H. *Cherokee Indian Nation a Troubled History*. University of Tennessee Press, 1979.

King, Elisha Sterling. *The Wild Rose of Cherokee*. Privately published, 1938.

Kuttruff, Carl. "Fort Watauga (40CR4)." Tennessee Department of Conservation, Tennessee Division of Archaeology, July 1979.

Lester, William Stewart. *The Transylvania Colony*. S.R. Guard, 1935.

Library of Congress. "Thomas Jefferson Papers: A Finding Aid to the Collection in the Library of Congress." Manuscript Division, 2014. https://www.loc.gov.

McConnell Map Company and James McConnell. "McConnell's Historical Maps of the United States." McConnell Map Company, 1919. Available via Library of Congress, https://www.loc.gov.

McGill, John T. "Andrew Greer." *Tennessee Historical Magazine* 2, no. 3 (September 1916): 204–07. https://www.jstor.org/stable/42637978.

McGill, John T., and Maggie H. Stone. "Joseph Greer: Kings Mountain Messenger." *Tennessee Historical Magazine* 2, no. 1 (March 1916): 40–42. https://www.jstor.org/stable/42637963.

Merritt, Frank. *Early History of Carter County, 1760–1861*. Archer & Smith, 1950.

Moore, Arthur K. *The Frontier Mind: A Cultural Analysis of the Kentucky Frontiersman*. Originally published 1957. Reprint, Lexington: University of Kentucky, 1957.

Moore, David G., Robin A. Beck, and Christopher B. Rodning. "Joara and Fort San Juan: Culture Contact at the Edge of the World." *Antiquity* Volume 78, Issue 299 (March 2004).

Moore, John Trotwood, and Austin P Foster. *Tennessee: The Volunteer State*. S.J. Clarke, 1923. Available via HathiTrust, https://www.hathitrust.org.

Morriss, Mack. *Watauga: The Dangerous Example*. Watauga Historical Association, 1974.

Moss, Bobby Gilmer. *Uzal Johnson, Loyalist Surgeon*. Scotia Hibernia Press, 2000.

Moss, Bobby Gilmer, and Michael C. Scoggins. *African American Patriots in the Southern Campaign of the American Revolution*. Scotia Hibernia Press, 2004.

Museum of the Cherokee People. https://motcp.org.

Nakoff, Slade. "From Tidewater to Tennessee: The Structuring Influences of Virginia Schemata in the Settlement of East Tennessee." Master's thesis, East Tennessee State University, 2024. https://dc.etsu.edu/etd/4391.

Nance, Benjamin C., and Samuel D. Smith. "A Survey of Sites Related to the American Revolution and the War of 1812 in Tennessee." Tennessee Division of Archaeology, 2004.

National Park Service and Overmountain Victory Trail Association. "Overmountain Victory National Historic Trail." Accessed May 30, 2025. https://npshistory.com/publications/ovvi/brochures/undated1.pdf.

Pigati, Jeffrey S., Kathleen B. Springer, Jeffrey S. Honke, et al. "Independent Age Estimates Resolve the Controversy of Ancient Human Footprints at White Sands." *Science* 382, no. 6666 (October 5, 2023): 73–75. https://doi.org/10.1126/science.adh5007.

Powell, Jim. "Spark of Revolution: A Biography of Samuel Adams." July 4, 2000. https://www.libertarianism.org.

Ramsey, J.G.M. *Annals of Tennessee to the End of the Eighteenth Century*. Originally published by Walker & Jones,1853. Reprint, Overmountain Press, 1999.

Rocky Mount State Historic Site. Rocky Mount Historical Association, 2025. https://www.rockymountmuseum.com.

Roos, Dave. "How Early Humans First Reached the Americas: 3 Theories." History, July 14, 2023. https://www.history.com.

Roosevelt, Theodore. *The Winning of the West.* Vol. 1. Putnam, 1917.

Rosen, Jeffrey. *The Pursuit of Happiness*. Simon and Schuster, 2024.

Sampeck, Kathryn, Jonathan Thayn, and Howard H. Earnest Jr. "Geographic Information System Modeling of de Soto's Route from Joara to Chiaha: Archaeology and Anthropology of Southeastern Road Networks in the Sixteenth Century." *American Antiquity* 80 (2015): 46–66. https://doi.org/10.7183/0002-7316.79.4.46.

Saunders, William L. *The Colonial Records of North Carolina 1775–1776*. Originally published 1890. Reprint, Broadfoot Publishing, 1993.

Saunders, William L., ed. *The Colonial Records of North Carolina*[...]. Vol. 10. Josephus Daniels, 1890. Available via HathiTrust, https://www.hathitrust.org.

Selesky, Harold E., and Mark Mayo Boatner. *Encyclopedia of the American Revolution: Library of Military History*. Charles Scribner's Sons, 2006.

Sequoyah Birthplace Museum. "Sequoyah Birthplace Museum." https://sequoyahmuseum.org.

Shreve, Nathan K., Jay D. Franklin, Eileen G. Ernenwein, Maureen A. Hays, and Ilaria Patania. "An Arc of Interaction, a Flow of People, and Emergent Identity: Early Contact Period Archaeology and Early European Interactions in the Middle Nolichucky Valley of Upper East Tennessee." In *Contact, Colonialism, and Native Communities in the Southeastern United States*, edited by Edmond A. Boudreaux, Maureen Meyers, and Jay K. Johnson. University Press of Florida, 2020.

Slon, Viviane, Charlotte Hopfe, Clemens L. Weiss, et al. "Neandertal and Denisovan DNA from Pleistocene Sediments." *Science* 356, no. 6338 (April 27, 2017): 605–08. https://doi.org/10.1126/science.aam9695.

Smith, Lloyd Thomas. *Robert Carter of Corotoman, 1663–1732*. Foundation for Historic Christ Church, 2009.

Smith, Samuel D. "Summary of Archaeological Explorations at the Carter House (40CR5), Carter County, Tennessee." Division of Archaeology, Tennessee Department of Conservation, 1979.

Stoneberg Holt, Sierra Dawn. "Reinterpreting the 1882 Bison Population Collapse." *Rangelands* 40, no. 4 (August 2018): 106–14. https://doi.org/10.1016/j.rala.2018.05.004.

Summitt, April R. *Sequoyah and the Invention of the Cherokee Alphabet*. Bloomsbury, 2012.

Talbert, Charles G. Review of *William Tatham, 1752–1819: American Versatile* by G. Melvin Herndon. *Register of the Kentucky Historical Society* 72, no. 1 (January 1974): 80–82. https://www.jstor.org/stable/23378295.

Timberlake, Henry. *The Memoirs of Lieutenant Henry Timberlake: The Story of a Soldier, Adventurer, and Emissary to the Cherokees, 1756–1765*. Edited by Duane H. King. Museum of the Cherokee Indian Press, 2007.

University of Chicago Library. "Guide to the Reuben T. Durrett Collection of Shelby Family Papers 1742–1823." 2016. https://www.lib.uchicago.edu.

University of North Carolina, Chapel Hill. "Description by Robert Campbell of the Battle of King's Mountain." Documenting the American South. https://docsouth.unc.edu/csr/index.php/document/csr15-0280.

Van West, Carroll, and Tennessee Historical Society. *The Tennessee Encyclopedia of History & Culture*. Tennessee Historical Society, 1998.

Washington, George. *The Writings of George Washington from the Original Manuscript Sources, 1745–1799*, vol. 28, *December 5, 1784–August 30, 1786*. Edited by John C. Fitzpatrick. U.S. Government Printing Office, 1939. Available via HathiTrust, https://www.hathitrust.org.

Watauga Historical Association. "Minutes of Meeting of Incorporators, Watauga Historical Association." Elizabethton, Tennessee, 1962.

Western Carolina University. "Research Guides: Cherokee, Native American, & Indigenous Studies: Introduction to the Field." May 3, 2025. https://researchguides.wcu.edu/CherokeeStudies/intro.

Willerslev, Eske, Anders J. Hansen, Jonas Binladen, et al. "Diverse Plant and Animal Genetic Records from Holocene and Pleistocene Sediments." *Science* 300, no. 5620 (April 17, 2003): 791–95.

Williams, Samuel Cole. *The Admission of Tennessee into the Union*. Overmountain Press, 1994.

———. *Ann Robertson: An Unsung Tennessee Heroine*. Tennessee Historical Commission, 1944.

———. *Brigadier-General Nathaniel Taylor*. Watauga Press. 1940.

———. *Dawn of Tennessee Valley and Tennessee History*. Watauga Press, 1937.

———. *Early Travels in the Tennessee Country, 1540–1800*. 2nd ed. Originally published 1928. Reprint, Franklin Book Reprints, 1970.

———. "The First Volunteers from the 'Volunteer State.'" *Tennessee Historical Magazine* 8, no. 2 (July 1904).

———. "Henderson and Company's Purchase Within the Limits of Tennessee." *Tennessee Historical Magazine* 5, no. 1 (April 1919): 5–27. https://www.jstor.org/stable/42637407.

———. *History of the Lost State of Franklin*. Originally published 1924. Reprint, Overmountain Press, 1933.

———. *The Lincolns and Tennessee*. Watauga Press, 1942.

———. "Tatham's Characters Among the North American Indians." *Tennessee Historical Magazine* 7, no. 3 (1921): 174–79. https://www.jstor.org/stable/44702575.

———. *Tennessee During the Revolutionary War*. Originally published 1944. Reprint, University of Tennessee Press, 1974.

———. *William Tatham, Wataugan*. Watauga Press, 1947.

Woodman, H. "Report Covering the Excavation of Burial Cists, Elizabethton, Tennessee." Bureau of American Ethnology/Smithsonian Institution, 1927.

Woodward, Grace Steele. *The Cherokees*. University of Oklahoma Press, 1988.

ABOUT THE AUTHOR

Jennifer A. Bauer, an avid lover of history and nature with a special fondness for being in the mountains, is a three-time graduate of East Tennessee State University. Recently retired after a forty-three-year career with Tennessee State Parks, she first served as a ranger naturalist at Roan Mountain State Park and later as park manager at Sycamore Shoals State Historic Park.

She enjoys teaching biology at Northeast State Community College and sharing history through eighteenth- and nineteenth-century reenacting and interpretation and currently serves on the board of directors of Friends of Roan Mountain and the Rocky Mount Historical Association.

She has written numerous articles for the *Tennessee Conservationist* and is the author of five books, the most recent being *Wildlife, Wildflowers and Wild Activities: Exploring Southern Appalachia* and *Roan Mountain: History of an Appalachian Treasure*.